IMMIGRANT CONCEPTS
LIFE PATHS TO INTEGRATION

Immigrant Concepts is Also Available in
Arabic as

مفاهيم المهاجر :
مسارات حياة الاندماج

German as *Immigrant Konzepte: Lebenswege zur Integration*

Spanish as *Inmigrante Conceptos: Vías de la Vida Hacia la Integración*

Forthcoming Books in this Series

Immigrant Psychology: Heart, Mind, and Soul
Immigrant Health & Wellness

IMMIGRANT CONCEPTS

LIFE PATHS TO INTEGRATION

Joachim O. F. Reimann, Ph.D.
Dolores I. Rodríguez-Reimann, Ph.D.

Romo Books

Immigrant Concepts: Life Paths to Integration

©2021, Joachim O. F. Reimann and Dolores I. Rodríguez-Reimann.

All rights reserved.

Published by Romo Books, Chula Vista, California

ISBN 978-1-955658-00-3 (paperback)
ISBN 978-1-955658-01-0 (eBook)
Library of Congress Control Number: 2021912415

Publisher's Cataloging-In-Publication Data
(Prepared by The Donohue Group, Inc.)

Names: Reimann, Joachim O. F., author. | Rodríguez-Reimann, Dolores Isabel, author.
Title: Immigrant concepts : life paths to integration / Joachim O.F. Reimann, Ph.D. [and]
Dolores I. Rodríguez-Reimann, Ph.D.
Description: Chula Vista, California : Romo Books, [2021] | Includes index.
Identifiers: ISBN 9781955658003 (paperback) | ISBN 9781955658010 (ebook)
Subjects: LCSH: Immigrants--Cultural assimilation. | Emigration and immigration--
Social aspects. | Social integration. | Immigrants--Employment. | Immigrants--Health
and hygiene. | Emigration and immigration--Psychological aspects.
Classification: LCC JV6342 .R45 2021 (print) | LCC JV6342 (ebook) | DDC
305.906912--dc23

Earth Cover Image Credit: Meteosat-3 & Meteosat-4 Observe the Earth (1993)/ESA,
CC BY-SA 3.0 IGO
https://www.esa.int/ESA_Multimedia/Copyright_Notice_Images
Phases of Adjustment Graphic adapted from Hurt D. 2000 Refugee Adaptation in the
Resettlement Process, The National Alliance for Multicultural Mental Health

Publishing consultant: David Wogahn, AuthorImprints.com

For Beate, Bernhard, Felipe and Héctor

CONTENTS

PREFACE

By Dolores I. Rodríguez-Reimann, Ph.D.

Some say that *intention* is an aim, a goal if you will, that guides action, purpose, or objective. Wikipedia describes it as a mental state that represents a commitment to carry out one or more actions.

My intentions in writing this book are two-fold. The first is an act of love; a way to narrate and honor my own life's journey as well as the journeys of my husband, many of my relatives, my friends, my colleagues, and my patients. As such, I want to give you, the reader, a framework that helps foster a better understanding of the many pieces that make up an immigration experience.

Secondly, with the help of my husband and life partner Joachim, I hope to present you with a model that spells out and integrates the most salient psychosocial dimensions involved. From that perspective, we want to highlight the many strengths immigrants bring with our experience. We also offer suggestions, recommendations, and ways to overcome barriers to successful integration into new environments.

By Joachim (Joe) O. F. Reimann, Ph.D.

I clearly remember my first night, at age ten, in the United States. Though tired after many hours of across-the-Atlantic travel, my family and I spent that night in a Los Angeles hotel room watching *Gunsmoke* on television. Of course it was in English so my mother and I understood very little of the dialogue. But the show was still fascinating. As we headed to our new home on the following day, a scary but also intriguing and entirely new world surrounded us.

At a very personal level, these memories prompt my interest in the ways migration shapes us. Dolores and I share the bond of love, marriage, and partnership. We are also both immigrants. Yet our personal experiences are different in terms of culture, country, distances we traveled, and socioeconomic circumstances we came from. Dolores lived closer to the US as she grew up in Mexico and was thus more familiar with American culture.

In short, the specific journeys people take can vary greatly. But Dolores and I share many similarities in our immigration experience. I hope our stories will help us speak to people from many different backgrounds across the immigration spectrum. As with Dolores, I intend to offer information about how immigrants can adapt to, and be successful in their new homes. That benefits all of us.

1

INTRODUCTION
PEOPLE ON THE MOVE

Humans have sought out new places to live for as long as we've been on the planet. Whether it was our migration out of East Africa roughly 70,000 years ago, Polynesians navigating thousands of miles across the open Pacific Ocean to discover new islands, Europeans arriving in the Americas, Cuban refugees reaching the coast of Florida, so-called "boat people" leaving Vietnam, or executives relocating to a new country as part of their international business, our travels have been never-ending.

Many journeys are chronicled in ancient texts like the Torah and the Bible as well as stories and tales of peoples across the world. In Mexico, for example, a legend of the Nahua people tells us that seven different tribes who shared a common language left their homeland ("*Chicomoztoc*") and settled near the mythical city of *Aztlán*. While scholars debate the exact location of *Aztlán*, legend has it that the city was ruled by ruthless leaders who called themselves *Azteca*. Consequently, the Nahua left again based on prophecy and divine guidance by their god *Huitzilopochtli*. The prophecy they followed said they would travel until they came across a site where they would then build a great city. The Nahua would know the site's location when they saw the signal: an eagle with a snake in its beak perched atop a cactus in the middle of a lake. The prophecy was fulfilled, and Tenochtitlan became the capital of the Mexican civilization and the Mexica people.

Other well-known stories include various migrations in the Asian world. These include the flight of refugees from countries like Vietnam and Kampuchea to Australia during the 1970s and 1980s.

Journeys have also become a standard backdrop in mythology and our popular literature. They are described in classics like Hercules and Beowulf to modern cinema (for example Luke Skywalker). Typical heroes start somewhat innocent and inexperienced. But by facing a multitude of physical and mental challenges on a quest they emerge changed for the better and often (though not always) triumphant.[1,2]

As chronicled in such legends, religious texts, and historical accounts, many reasons prompt us to migrate. These include the search for a better life and future, economic and career opportunities, religious and political freedom, a flight from violence caused by war and persecution, and a desire to escape densely populated areas for a place with fewer people and the hardship that comes with stretched resources. In short, people from a multitude of social, cultural, economic, ethnic, religious, and other circumstances migrate.

The desire to find increased opportunities is one reason someone might migrate. But others are forced to escape their country because of war, persecution, climate change, and threats from criminal gangs. To remain at home could mean that they and/or their loved ones will be enslaved or killed. The bottom line: some of us migrate to seek opportunities and some of us migrate because we see no other choice.

The number of people migrating worldwide has grown quickly in recent years. According to the United Nations' Department of Economic and Social Affairs, there were around 272 million international migrants in 2019. This is an increase of 14 million since 2017 and 51 million since 2010. As such worldwide migrants comprise roughly 3.5% of the global population.[3]

Displaced persons fleeing their homes make up a significant number of this population. At the time this book was written, forced migration patterns were driven by on-going conflicts of various types in the Middle East, East Africa, Latin America, and other locations. The UN Refugee Agency, for example, estimates that 79.5 million people worldwide were forcibly displaced at the end of 2019.[4]

More specifically, refugees from countries in the greater Middle East (e.g. Syria, Afghanistan, and Southern Sudan) make up a significant number of the world's refugees. In the case of the Syrian civil war, more than half that country's population has been forced to flee their homes since 2011. This includes roughly 6.6 million refugees who are seeking safety in neighboring countries (e.g., Lebanon, Jordan, Turkey, Iraq, and Egypt).[5]

European Union (EU) countries have also been a major destination. The International Organization for Migration (IOM) estimates that around 1,046,600 migrants came to the EU in 2015, roughly 766,600 more than in 2014.[6] Much of this trend continues. As per Eurostat, the number of first-time asylum applicants in the EU in 2019 was 612,700.[7]

The EU and the Middle East are not the only places with large recent numbers of displaced persons. The United Nations Network on Migration, for example, estimates that about five million people left Venezuela due to socioeconomic instability and political turmoil by mid-2020. This is the largest external displacement crisis in Latin America's recent history. Most of the Venezuelans have remained in South America (Columbia, Peru, Chile, Ecuador, and Brazil). But that puts an additional burden on those countries as well.[8]

It is of particular concern that about 30–34 million (38–43%) half of the world's forcibly displaced persons are children under 18 years of age.[4] Some of these minors travel alone (without their parents or relatives). This is an obvious concern and demonstrates how forced displacement has impacted young lives.

The United States has also felt the influx of persons from other countries. Many of these came from African and Middle Eastern locations. In 2015 roughly 46% self-identified as Muslim, the highest annual percentage on record. Others identified as Christians (44%), other religions, or without religious adherence. As per the US Census Bureau, net international migration to the US decreased from 1,047,000 between 2015 and 2016 to 595,000 to the US population between 2018 and 2019.[9] But while trends around immigration vary over time, history suggests that worldwide migration will continue unabated.

Popular attention to specific groups often shifts. Recent reports in the US media have focused on caravans coming from Central American migrants. They are also known as the *Via Crucis del Migrante* ("Migrant's Way of the Cross").[10] These caravans include large groups of people who travel from the Guatemala–Mexico border to the Mexico–United States border. The majority are from the Northern Triangle of Central America (Guatemala, El Salvador, and Honduras).

The best known and largest caravans were reportedly organized by *Pueblo Sin Fronteras* (Village without Borders). Experts have debated the makeup of people in these caravans. Some believe that they are largely comprised of refugees seeking asylum. Numerous human rights organizations have documented violence and abuse in Central America. A 2019 report by the International Committee of the Red Cross, for example, reminds us that armed violence rates in El Salvador, Honduras, and Guatemala remain some of the highest in the world.[11]

Other people working on the topic argue that these immigrants are comprised of large concentrations of traditional economic migrants. The causes of the migration, as well as the proper way to settle or deport the migrants remains a source of much political debate within the US and other countries around the world. This includes complexities about what meets legal asylum requirements.

It is also worth remembering that immigration does not only involve people escaping bad situations. Eurostat reports that in 2018, 2.6 million non-EU citizens obtained the right to both live and work in the EU through business-related permits.[12]

The US the State Department notes that every fiscal year, approximately 140,000 employment-based immigrant visas are issued. Additionally, 389,579 student visas were issued in the US during 2018.[13]

All of the numbers cited above can feel overwhelming—millions here and millions there. We present them to make one main point: Immigration is an important issue that impacts many lives requiring broader society's proactive, thoughtful, objective and on-going attention.

Migrating to a new country presents both challenges and potential benefits to the immigrants and to the new county they are entering. In the best circumstances, an influx of new populations has the potential to vitalize host countries with unfamiliar but vibrant human energy and potential. Conversely, immigration failures result in burdens and hardships on both the migrants themselves and the greater society. We provide some detailed examples in later chapters.

In short, this migration of people, particularly when they come in large numbers, has to be managed well by host countries as well as international support systems. There have to be collaborative and coordinated efforts. Otherwise, social infrastructures can become overwhelmed. In this context it is important to say that any system can become overpowered when the number of immigrants simply exceeds its capacity. As such it does not make sense to have an entirely open-door approach. But migration is a reality that societal views of the moment are unlikely to change. We need to deal with that reality in the most effective way possible.

This book presents an overview of key essentials we believe can help immigrants succeed in their adaptation to a new society. Our twenty years of professional work in psychological theory and clinical practice, public health, and other research (cultural competence, forensic evaluations), and workforce development provide the backdrop of our expertise in helping immigrants adapt to their new home. But equally important, it draws on our personal and family immigration stories. We believe this book will be useful to immigrants as well as the professionals and others who work directly with them. In addition, we hope that it will help shape immigration policy.

In the following pages, we provide you, the reader, with information about demographic trends and describe psycho-social concepts involved in the immigration experience. We have combined these concepts into an integrated model that can help to create successful integration. We will share some brief vignettes and stories to illustrate the points we are describing.

Finally, at the end of each section, we pose questions for you to think about your own experience, the experience of a loved one, or a friend, co-worker or client. As you read through the book, we hope that we can provide you with wisdom and practical information to help you in your journey and provide you the safe and informative space that will allow you to think about your experiences of success and your struggles. No book on immigration would be complete without the suggestions and recommendations we provide that are sure to help you navigate the sometimes-tricky world of immigration. We've walked the walk and want to pass that on.

Before we begin, a few points of clarification:

In some parts of this book, we describe symptoms associated with certain types of psychiatric disorders. This is based on our clinical experience working with people who have a trauma history or other relevant circumstances. But such descriptions cannot be used to diagnose or treat you. That can only be done by a professional who you work with directly. So, if you find yourself worrying about any or all of the concepts described in this book, please address them with a mental health provider. If you are not connected with a therapist, speak to your primary care medical doctor who can make the appropriate recommendations and referrals for treatment if needed.

Throughout this text, we will highlight concepts and issues that are "typical" of the immigrant experience as cited in the research literature. But we fully recognize that we are all individuals with our own distinct story to tell. Immigrants, as a group, have as much within-group diversity as any other group.

In this book, we use several terms including "migrants," "immigrants," "refugees," and "asylum seekers." Often, the media also uses the word "foreigners" about immigrants. We do not use this last term extensively but will define all the terms in the book's glossary for clarification. For now, and to make it easier, we will define eight of the most frequently used terms below. We endeavor to use all of these terms and descriptions respectfully.

Foreigner is often used to describe a person from outside of one's country. While not always the case, the term is sometimes used in a negative or derogatory context. (To be discussed in more detail later).

An *Immigrant* is a person who has come to live permanently in a country that is not his or her place of birth and/or citizenship. The key here is the word "permanently." As such, it does not apply to people who are tourists or who visit a foreign county for work temporarily.

A *Migrant* is a person who is in the process of moving between one place or country and another (except for tourists and other very temporary travelers). This is sometimes applied to people who come to a foreign country to work (e.g., migrant farmworkers) with the possible intent to periodically return home.

Refugee refers to people who have been forced to migrate out of their country of origin because of threats on their lives and danger to themselves. This term is tricky because it is sometimes broadly applied to any immigrant who was forced to migrate. But on a more formal basis, it tends to refer to a specific legal status. For example, according to title VIII of the United States Code Section 1100 and 1A 42, a refugee is *an alien who is unable or unwilling to return to his or her country because of persecution, or a well-founded fear of persecution, on account of race, religion, nationality, membership in a particular social group, or political opinion.* An individual cannot qualify for this status if he or she has persecuted others, has been firmly resettled in a third country or has been convicted of certain serious crimes (e.g., felonies, smuggling, engaging in domestic violence). The specific legal parameters dictating refugee status tend to vary from country to country.[14]

Asylum is a term used in the context of refugees who have been granted a specific legal immigration status in a country they have entered. To be granted asylum people have to show that they were persecuted in the past, or that they have a well-founded fear of being persecuted in the future should they return to the country of origin. Given that people who flee their homes, often in a hurry, do not tend to have much formal documentation about the physical and or psychological threats they were under back home, proving such circumstances in a court can be challenging.

Home Country is the country that people originated from (e.g., by birth, citizenship, etc.)

The *Host Country* is the new country immigrants have entered.

Foreign Students are those who come to study in a foreign country under a particular educational visa. In the US, foreign students will have either an F-1 or M-1 visa. Students who study in a country other than their own often do so with the premise that they will return home when the studies are done.

One other note regarding language and terms: We know that people are a sum of all of their identities. We respect all identities such as gay, bisexual, gender-neutral, or queer without prejudice. Sexual orientation is a factor that can influence many elements of migration (and will be addressed in parts of this book). We are aware that the term *Latinx* has become a preference among some people of Latin American origins. These individuals prefer the term because it presents a gender-neutral or non-binary alternative to Latino or Latina. We, however, are also aware that this term has not been recognized by a significant part of the Latino/Latina community.[15] We thus use the terms Latino/Latina in this book but acknowledge the complexities of identity without exception.

We also use the term "Black" rather than "African-American" to refer to darker-skinned people, of Sub-Saharan African origins or descent. The two primary reasons for doing so are as follows: First, our text has an international focus while "African-American" is a more US-specific term. Secondly, "African-American" is largely associated with the US history of slavery and does not connect with the experience of recent migrants coming to the US from various parts of Africa. We understand that there is not yet a full consensus as to which term African origin people in the US prefer.

Throughout the book, we will use vignettes (personal stories) to illustrate the points. These vignettes do not disclose any identifying information of the people we have worked or collaborated with. Rather, they are an amalgam of our experience and knowledge. None of the names used throughout this book (other than our own or family members from whom we have permission) identify specific people. The names are used for illustration only and any resemblance to people, dead or alive, is purely coincidental.

2

SUCCESSFUL INTEGRATION
A BRIEF OVERVIEW

A dapting to new circumstances can be stressful, even under the best of circumstances. Let's say you've just bought a new home. It's beautiful—the one you've always wanted. On moving day, you find yourself sitting among a ton of boxes. Nothing is organized yet; nothing is set up; finding things—even if the boxes are labeled—is a challenge and can feel frustrating. And exactly what happened to the toiletries?

Moving disrupts routines in unfamiliar surroundings. Not surprisingly, this can cause some distress. Now imagine that you're not moving across town but to a new country. You don't know where anything is and how anything works and often your new neighbors are using a language you don't understand. This can raise a number of questions: How do you fit into your new country? Will it be too difficult? Will the local people accept you? Will you lose part or all of your core identity if you adapt to this new place?

An additional stressor can be employment and education. Will people in your new country accept your education and experience? Some immigrants have very little if any schooling. Even when people are highly skilled, seasoned, and educated (like physicians or attorneys), host countries may not readily accept their credentials. If you were recruited by an employer to work in a new country and your qualifications were vetted upfront through an E1 or E2 visa, work, and career goals, this is not a problem. But otherwise, finding work either as a professional or an unskilled laborer can be a significant barrier to successful adaptation to your new surroundings.

The scientific and clinical literature recognizes that culturally and linguistically distinct groups who migrate to a new country encounter psychosocial stressors, sometimes for more than one generation if problems encountered by the original immigrants linger. Even relatively minor relocations under positive circumstances can be demanding.[16] Not surprisingly, acculturating to a new country (e.g., acquiring a new language, adapting to different societal rules, changes in social status), is often innately stressful.[17]

Such difficulties have been acknowledged in formal diagnostic books that address psychological difficulties associated with migration. Starting with its fourth edition, the American Psychiatric Association's Diagnostics and Statistical Manual of Mental Disorders listed "acculturation stress" (DSM-IV-TR) and later "acculturation difficulty" (DSM 5) in the diagnostic terms it uses.[18,19]

The International Classification of Diseases, tenth edition (ICD-10) also has such a classification (Code Z60.3).[20] In some cases, such difficulties can spill over to second and third generations, especially if low socioeconomic status or social isolation persist.[21,22]

The experiences people bring with them to their new home can also be difficult. For example, considerable numbers of immigrants from the Middle East have been subjected to traumatic events including war, persecution, imprisonment, and torture in their countries of origin.[23] Similarly, many people coming from the Northern Triangle in Central America have experienced gang threats and violence. This can leave both physical and psychological scars.

A number of academics have proposed a model showing the steps immigrants tend to go through in their adjustment to a new country.[24]

A common representation of this model is as follows:

In the first "arrival" phase there may be excitement and fascination about being in a new place. If people have escaped dangerous circumstances, there can also be a relief and a sense of security. But some confusion about the new surroundings can also be present. In "Phase II" reality hits. This can involve a growing awareness that adjustment is difficult. Disappointment can set in, especially if the immigrant arrived with unrealistic notions of the benefits a new country has to offer. Phase II can also be impacted by experiences in which the immigrant is discriminated against based on their origins, ethnicity, race, and other factors. Reactions to these circumstances range from fear and anger to frustration. In addition, many immigrants may feel the loss of their country of origin. How well new immigrants cope with the Phase II "reality check" has a significant impact on their later success. In this process family stability and support, health, and personal resilience all foster positive outcomes. How well people cope in Phase II can lead to a future that is freer of emotional and physical burdens and less hesitation to try new endeavors such as finding work, making friends, and enjoying life in general.

Phase III really involves two alternate paths. One, often labeled "negotiation" involves the immigrant taking the initiative, developing social networks, learning new skills (e.g.,

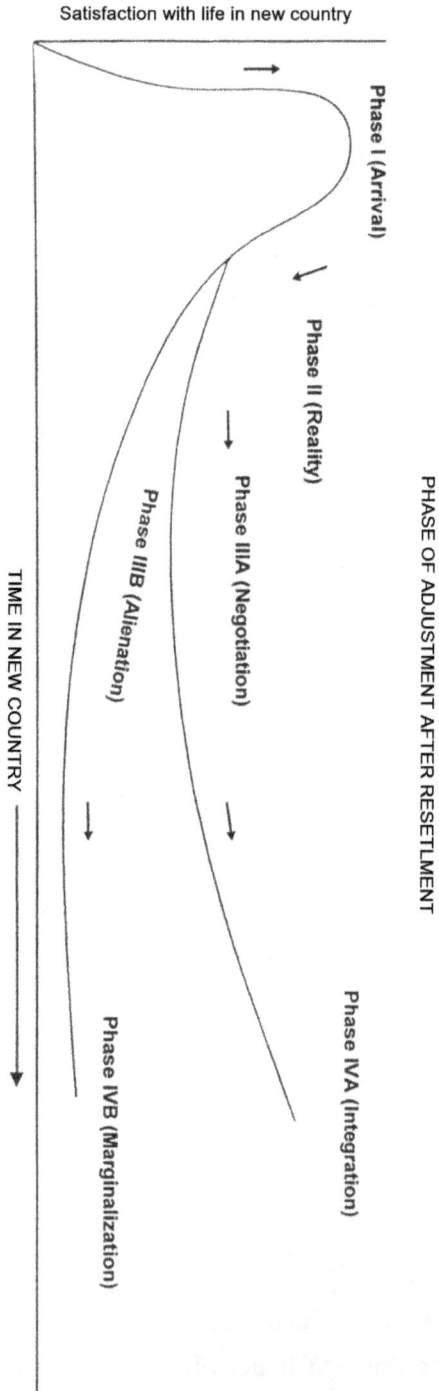

Satisfaction with life in new country

TIME IN NEW COUNTRY

PHASE OF ADJUSTMENT AFTER RESETLMENT

Phase I (Arrival)

Phase II (Reality)

Phase IIIA (Negotiation)

Phase IIIB (Alienation)

Phase IVA (Integration)

Phase IVB (Marginalization)

language), and finding positive social roles to take on. On the negative side, "alienation" involves becoming withdrawn, desperate, and apathetic. Not surprisingly, this path ultimately leads to family dysfunctions, dependence on others, unemployment, and, in some cases, even legal problems.

"Integration," the more positive path, has the potential to lead to better psychological and social adjustment, increased self-sufficiency, self-confidence, useful skills, and a more hopeful outlook toward the future.

In the following chapters, this book addresses in greater detail concepts we believe are important to successful integration. We discuss education, economic, physical and mental health, and other social circumstances. We also address potential barriers to success, the importance of resilience, and recommendations of how barriers can be overcome through personal strengths and the ability to build social networks and supports. In that process, it is important to remember that, as immigrants, we don't necessarily have to give up who we are at our core to "successfully integrate" or adjust to our new homes.

Questions you may wish to consider:

- As you think about your own immigration experience or that of a loved one:
- What are the factors, memories, and experiences that remain most important to you?
- Was it the journey itself?
- How long did this process take?
- What experiences did you have along the way?
- How would you describe your process of integration into your new life?
- Do you believe you have been successful?

- If you had to do it all over again, would you do anything differently? (If so, what?)
- Are there insights and wisdom that others can learn from your experience?

3

INTEGRATION
FACTORS AND CHALLENGES

When you hear people in the media talk about what path leads to success for immigrants, words like "assimilation," and "melting pot" are often used. In this context assimilation, as thought of in the past, implies that 1) you have to give up your identity—who you are at your core—and become a "new you" in your adopted country and 2) the "new you" has to fit into the predominate culture found in that country. A "melting pot" suggests that all people, including those who are native-born to that country, change to fit a changing cultural norm.

The idea that people will be required to change who they are and how they see themselves in the world can be scary. Psychologists tell us that much of our identity is made up of the social groups we identify as being part of. When asked "who are you?" we tend to respond with classifications such as gender and/or sexual orientation (man/woman/transgender/gay/straight/bi, etc.) family roles (e.g., husband/wife/father/mother), political affiliations, ethnicity/race, religious affiliation, tribal membership, profession or, most commonly, a combination of these (e.g., a Black female engineer). All of these are social groups. Even our names tend to identify our ethnic and national origins. For example, "Rogelio" is a Spanish given name; "Hans" is of Germanic origins (although it is also common in Danish, Dutch, Norwegian, Icelandic, and Swedish-speaking countries). What you call yourself is central to who you are. The thought that we may have to change that to fit in somewhere is often distressing.

Even if we have a strong educational and economic background there are challenges. The degree of your effort to change and adapt will depend on where you come from and where you go to. Learning a new language is not easy for most of us, no matter our personal history. But even if your new country uses your native language, you will likely encounter many different traditions, norms, and requirements. International students, for example, tend to have stress connected with foreign academic environments.[25] As we address in later chapters, your chosen profession will likely have different rules and regulations in a new country.

There are also other less immediately obvious yet very important differences between countries. Various medications are not approved for use in all locations. Laws around driving, privacy, and smoking may be different. Polite etiquette will most certainly vary. The list goes on.

One piece of good news is that, while you may have to change how you do some things, you don't necessarily have to change how you see yourself at a basic level. Researchers who delve into immigration issues often use the term "acculturation" (sometimes referred to as "enculturation"). Another frequently used term is "ethnic identity." While there is some overlap between these concepts, they are not automatically the same thing.

We discuss these concepts in detail below. But in a nutshell, acculturation focuses more on the skills and habits we adopt in a new society. Typical examples include language, understanding the laws and rules of society, road signs, and so on. The term "ethnic identity" focuses more on how we see and identify ourselves at our core.

Acculturation

Acculturation is formally defined as a phenomenon that results when groups of individuals having different cultures come into continuous and direct contact. This leads to subsequent changes in the original cultural patterns of either and/or both groups. In other words, it's when an immigrant begins to acquire and adjust to the norms of their adoptive country. At the most basic level, it characterizes an individual's process of cultural change.[26]

In short, acculturation, particularly on the psychological level, involves the dynamic adaptation to the culture of the new country. It occurs in the context of local communities, economic circumstances, and a host of other factors. Acculturation can change many aspects of immigrants' lives. Often one major change is learning a new language. But basic attitudes, political views, economic status, personal values, dietary preferences, what entertainment people enjoy, and what customs people engage in can also evolve. Acculturation is not, however, a "one size fits all" process. As described below, there are many ways in which it can happen. Much of this depends on the characteristics of an individual and the new social climate an immigrant finds in his or her new country.[25]

Acculturation normally happens in stages and is influenced, in large part, by a person's age. According to research, children learn a new language more quickly than their adult counterparts. They may also be able to more readily speak a new language without an accent. In contrast, this may be much more difficult for older adults.

Typically people also tend to learn a new language first and then pursue other opportunities to build broader societal connections (since such opportunities open up with language skills). There are instances, however, in which immigrants have lived in their new country for an extended time and still do not acquire the local language. In such cases, they tend to live in communities made up of people from similar origins, making it possible for them to get by in their new country while maintaining strong identification with the values of their original culture. Because they are around people who speak the language they know, older immigrants may retain much of their original ethnic and national identities. Not learning the language of their adopted country, however, means they are less able to access the full opportunities their new home offers.

As partly shown above, acculturation (or choosing not to acculturate) is a complex and multi-faceted psychological phenomenon. In the past, it was thought to require that a person must let go of old ways of thinking and acting in order to adapt to their new country. Today, evolving philosophies about the acculturation processes, take into consideration the many paths an immigrant can take to feel at home in their new country. One basic model proposed by John Berry[27] and widely adopted is as follows:

Acculturation Model		
	Tends to Maintain Country of Origin Norms	Does not Maintain Country of Origin Norms
Tends to Learn and Adopt New Country Norms	Integrated (Bicultural)	Assimilated
Does not Learn and Adopt New Country Norms	Separated from Broader Society Remains Traditional to country of origin	Marginalized (or develops something entirely new)

Looking at these four potential boxes, possible acculturation (or acculturation to a lesser degree) outcomes are as follows:

Assimilation in this context means that immigrants have let go of norms and practices associated with the country they come from and have replaced these practices with those of their new country. This is essentially the old view of integration: the belief that, by definition, people have to leave behind traditions from the home country to learn new ones. Research has now shown that this is not the only path in acculturation. However, it might be a strategy for people who believe their migration represents a clean break from the past and a new beginning for a better future. It may also be adopted by those who are at odds with common beliefs in their home country and/or who were persecuted for their different beliefs. Issues like the similarity between the country of origin and the new environment (same language, similarities in religion) as well as historical political circumstances, (such as escaping a society that is now at war with the new host country) during immigration may also play a role in whether an immigrant chooses to assimilate. Immigrant parents may view assimilation as a safer option for their children. It is also likely that, across all immigrant families, assimilation becomes predominant with every new generation. Children are more likely to assimilate than their parents, and then the children's children carry that process further.

To fully understand assimilation, it is also important to consider history. In the US during the 18th Century, for example, immigrants were expected to assimilate and fit into mainstream American life, making assimilation a forced construct for immigration.

Separation is essentially the opposite of assimilation and involves a relatively limited degree of acculturation. This is sometimes referred to being "traditional." It occurs when immigrants chooses to maintain the norms of their original country and do not adopt the practices of their new country. There are many reasons for such an outcome. Some people who undergo forced migration may believe that they will eventually return to their country of origin. For instance, war or violence may have forced them to leave. But they hold onto the norms of their home country, thinking they will return when the situation "back home" has calmed down.

Some may also believe that learning a new language is just too hard, and only feel safe when surrounded by others from their home country or may feel that some practices of the country in which they find themselves run contrary to their moral or religious beliefs. The result can be ethnic neighborhoods that isolate immigrants from broader society. While the comfort of the familiar is understandable, this option is also limiting in terms of economic success and general participation in broader society.

Marginalization is a term frequently used with immigrants who neither maintain their traditional social norms nor adopt those of their new country. A common, though often incorrect assumption is that people find themselves essentially belonging in no clear category. But some people, particularly within the younger generations, have developed new personal expressions that are not automatically evident in their home country or their new society. As mentioned earlier, the process of acculturation continues across generations and can take new forms with immigrants' children. Unique circumstances can develop in that context. For example, in 1940s Mexican-American culture, some younger people wore Zoot Suits, a unique fashion that may have been derived from Black communities (particularly jazz musicians). This style was not common in Mexico or the broader United States. Similarly, in the Chicano lowrider culture, people customize classic cars in unique ways. The mainstream United States and Mexican traditions do not have this form of expression. (We suspect that finding a lowrider in Mexico City would be difficult.) In short, some people adopt this acculturative strategy—inventing their own expressive customs as an immigrant culture—to develop a new and unique identity for themselves.

Integration, sometimes called biculturalism, is a strategy in which individuals keep relevant practices from their country of origin and also adopt practices from their new country. In other words, people maintain some degree of home-culture integrity while, at the same time, they learn how to participate as a vital part of their new country's larger social network. This has the potential to be a "best of both worlds" approach. Being well-versed in two or more cultures brings access to resources that are useful in a range of settings. Becoming bilingual or even multilingual is a good example of integration. It has the potential to enhance your success since speaking multiple languages is highly prized in certain parts of the world. Of course, some aspects of becoming bicultural are easier and some are harder. Learning to read the street signs might be relatively easy. You don't forget how to read the ones in your country of origin in that process. But negotiating two different religions (in the case of immigrating to a country where the predominant religion is markedly different than your own) is less viable.

What motivates people to use one of these options? Why are some people more willing to take on the customs and practices of their adopted country while others are not? A few reasons have already been discussed above. But there are many more circumstances to think about. Research in this area continues to expand our knowledge. Please see a few resources on the topic at the end of this chapter.

In summary, acculturation can be described as the process during which an immigrant learns (or does not learn) a set of skills that will be necessary to successfully integrate into the new broader society. The process influences many aspects of an immigrant's life. This includes how illnesses, including mental illnesses, and health services are perceived. It also includes how immigrants are received by the general public. We will address acculturation and physical as well as mental health perceptions and care in later chapters. But one particular, most directly related aspect of mental health is as follows.

Acculturation Stress

A process that requires people to learn new and different skills, many of which include subtle nuances that can be extremely challenging, often cause stress. One possible result of acculturation, then, is an accumulation of worries and anxiety. This leads us to the concept of "acculturative stress." Such stress is defined as a marked deterioration of the general health status of an individual. It encompasses physiological, psychological, and social aspects that are explicitly linked to the acculturation process. The degree of acculturated stress experienced by an individual can range from mild tensions which gradually improve as the individual adapts, to debilitating stress that worsens over time. Most commonly, individuals experiencing acculturative stress display symptoms of anxiety and depression which may increase without an effective social support system.

As noted in Chapter 2, acculturative stress has been acknowledged in formal diagnostic books that address psychological difficulties associated with migration. "Acculturation stress" and "acculturation difficulty" have been used as a diagnostic terms (DSM-5).[19] The intensity of acculturative stress tends to depend on the similarities or differences between immigrants' country of origin and their new country. This includes the new host culture's political and social attitudes, especially towards the newcomers. Not surprisingly, the more radically different the host culture is compared to the newcomer's native culture, the more acculturative stress will probably be experienced.[28]

Overall, for an immigrant who is highly sought after because of professional expertise and/or who "looks like" the local population (because the home country and new country have similar languages, traditions, religion, and ethnic composition) acculturation may be a comparatively easier proposition. On the other hand, people who look "different," who come from lower socioeconomic circumstances, or whose knowledge and expertise are not accepted in their new country (e.g., foreign-trained physicians) tend to have more obstacles to overcome.

As previously noted, there are also generational components to acculturation. Younger people usually have an easier time learning a new language and adapting to new environments. The fact that they become the ones helping older relatives navigate society can upset traditional family power roles. Families that come from more conservative cultures may also be upset and feel disrespected when their children adopt more liberal practices in their new country. While, generally, developing adolescents often challenge and upset parents during the most stable of times, when cognitive changes of the adolescent coincide with immigration, the imbalance in family dynamics can be more pronounced. The acculturative process, as noted earlier, can stretch across several generations, with each acting in age and time-specific realities.

Given the above, immigrant parents and children may increasingly live in what amounts to different worlds. Parents often have little understanding of their children's lives outside the home. On the other hand, children are faced with juggling the expectations of one culture in the home and another one at school. This may leave them hesitant to bring up any problems with their parents because those parents don't know a new culture well enough to provide "good advice." Children may also worry about putting additional stress on their parents.

Research has found connections between Latino adolescents' language acquisition, family, and broader society. On average, those who had learned less English were seen more favorably (essentially as better children) by their immediate family and friends while those who had learned more English had more positive experiences in all other areas of life such as school.[29] The loss of family closeness can be a source of stress for adolescents. The feeling that they have to decide between family and success in the broader world is not an easy choice for them. Parents can be upset if they feel left behind by their children. Children then pick up on that distress which can make them anxious.

Acculturated stress also tends to be severe among refugees. But their experience is not unique. For example, the acculturative stress levels reported by international students can approach that of refugees, which might be surprising at first. This may be the result of international students most likely having limited personal resources when they enter a host country. Their experience as students also might cause multiple overlapping challenges since, in addition to facing general acculturation issues, students confront traditional academic stresses. This stress is exacerbated because they tend to lack the personal support systems domestic students can tap into. The combined effect of the stressors, coupled with the possible lack of resources available to assist international students and the transition to the whole society, make the students highly susceptible to the harmful effects of acculturative stress. In addition to experiencing a greater proportion of illness related to stress, international students tend not to seek psychological help for fear of the stigma. This again exacerbates the problem.[25]

In summary, it is no surprise that acculturation can be stressful. The research literature has linked it to emotional difficulties (e.g. depression, anxiety, and loneliness), substance abuse, physical problems, strains on family relations, and other struggles. There is also significant evidence that some groups are more severely impacted than others. One such factor is whether or not a person's migration was voluntary or not. Involuntary migrants experience about 50% more acculturative stress than those who left their country of origin under more positive circumstances.

As previously described, family dynamics can be also stressful, as well as the negative reactions immigrants might experience by people in the broader society. We will discuss that in the "discrimination" section below.

What can help make acculturation less stressful? Research has linked less worry with younger age at migration and higher levels of education. Some studies have also found that a desire or at least a willingness to acculturate can reduce stress.[30] Efforts by broader society to develop comprehensive, organized, and integrated social systems that help newcomers be successful would contribute to a solution.

Acculturation is not, however, the only challenge that immigrants face when they interact with their new culture. Another element is how we identify ourselves at our core. This brings us to a discussion of ethnic identity.

Ethnic Identity

Dr. Jean Phinney, a leading expert in the area of ethnic identity, has defined it as *"an enduring, fundamental aspect of the self that includes a sense of membership in an ethnic group and the attitudes and feelings associated with that membership."*[31]

More informally, "ethnic identity" can be described as choosing to identify with groups to which we feel a kinship. For immigrants, identification often involves a recognition that, in their new society (like in most places around the world), what you call yourself and who you associate with can have a dramatic impact on how others treat you. That involves not only "learning rules of the game" (acculturation) but also understanding that the "rules apply differently depending on who you are."

Understanding the social power different groups wield in the greater society is part of an immigrants' decision-making and often directs the choices people make. Essentially social identity theory[32] notes that people have two basic ways to improve their wellbeing if, for example, they are members of a comparatively low-power / low resources group. They can either try to join a group with more power or find ways to increase their own group's power. Phenotype (e.g., skin color), ethnicity, language, accents, religion (e.g., those that require distinctive clothing), and other factors may make it difficult for people to be accepted into a dominant high-power group (essentially to "pass"). This leaves efforts to increase the power of ones' group as the remaining choice. Historically people have done so by trying a broad range of strategies. These have included advocacy through social media, art forms, like music and cinema, political advocacy, protests, marches, and even violence, which we don't endorse. Not surprisingly discrimination keeps people from gaining social power and standing.

Discrimination

The American Psychological Association (APA) defines discrimination as an unfair or prejudicial treatment of people and groups based on such characteristics as race, gender, age, or sexual orientation.[33] From a psychological perspective, discrimination is a public health issue. According to the 2020 Stress in America Survey, people who feel they have been discriminated against describe their stress levels as generally higher than those without such experiences.[34] Consequences can be physical and mental health problems including anxiety, depression, obesity, high blood pressure, and substance abuse. People can be negatively impacted, even if they have not personally faced discrimination. Just being part of a group that suffers discriminated can cause anxiety and worry. Moreover, the anticipation of discrimination creates its own chronic stress. People might avoid situations where they expect to be treated poorly, possibly missing out on educational and job opportunities.

What does discrimination look like among immigrants? Statistics from the EU show that North Africans (31%), Roma (sometimes called Gypsies) (26%), and sub-Saharan Africans (24%) report the most incidents because of their ethnic, racial, or immigrant background. Second-generation immigrants tend to report more incidents of discrimination, perhaps because they are more acculturated and thus more able to identify such incidents for what they are when they occur. Many of those impacted (71%) reported that they did not do not know who to turn to for help.[35]

The UK survey further showed that discrimination most commonly happens in healthcare (59%), employment or workplace (50%), and housing (36%) arenas. Most common acts of discrimination are statistically based on skin color and "foreign sounding" names. Such circumstances are personally distressing. But they also erode the potential sense of attachment immigrants feel to their new country and the level of trust they have in that country's institutions.[35]

Here is another example: In the US there are roughly 60.6 million Latinos as of 2019. About half are immigrants and another 23% are US-born adult children of immigrant parents. In these groups, 38% of adults report that they have personally experienced discrimination during the prior year. Incidents included being criticized for speaking Spanish in public, being told to go back to their home country, and being called offensive names.[36]

Sometimes, the basic fact that people are considered "foreigners" is enough to spark discrimination. In the US such a label often refers to migrants from Mexico, China, or the

Philippines. In the UK it commonly refers to people from India, Pakistan, Poland, and Ireland. Some research has shown that there is prejudice towards "foreigners" no matter where they come from. This may be driven by fears that they will take jobs and use social services at the expense of native-born citizens. Other studies have shown that people express more negative attitudes toward foreigners who are culturally different from the native population because they pose cultural threats.

Biases against newer arrivals and/or those who are less acculturated can occur, even within the same ethnic group. For example within some juvenile detention environments, Mexican-American adolescents who speak little or no English are looked down on and sometimes harassed by their more acculturated Mexican-American peers.

Not all of the statistics are dire. In the US roughly 30% of Latinos said someone had expressed support for them because of their Latino background.[36]

When people from all walks of life are supportive, it makes a huge difference. This is not limited to but certainly includes legal protections.

In developed countries, some laws designed to protect people from discrimination are in place. In the US, for example, the Fair Housing Act[37] prohibits discrimination in the sale, rental, and financing of dwellings based on race, color, national origin, religion, sex, familial status, and disability. The Civil Rights Act,[38] the Age Discrimination in Employment Act,[39] and the Americans with Disabilities Act[40] prohibit discrimination in employment based on race, color, sex, ethnic origin, age, and disabilities. While laws are important, they are not the whole story. Some violations are hard to prove in court. As described next, others are just difficult to recognize.

Some discrimination is blatantly obvious. But experts say that there are also smaller examples of day-to-day biases. Receiving poor service at stores or restaurants, being treated with a lack of courtesy and respect, or being treated as less intelligent or less trustworthy, may be more common than "obvious" discrimination. Sometimes termed "micro aggressions" these acts are more subtle. But they can be just as harmful to health and well-being as more overt acts. People who experience day-to-day discrimination often feel they're in a state of constant vigilance. That heightened watchfulness can generate chronic stress.[41]

A Word about "Perceived Discrimination"

If you read literature on the topic of discrimination, you may run across the term "perceived discrimination." In this context the word "perceived" is not meant to imply that people's experiences of discrimination and racism are untrue. More often, perceptions around discrimination are valid. If anything, discrimination may not be directly overt but can find more subtle expression like being excluded from housing or jobs based on race, gender, sexual orientation, etc. But the term "perceived" is sometimes used in research because it is perceptions or awareness of discrimination that tend to drive attitudes and behavioral strategies.

Our Own Stories:

In writing these chapters we use our professional knowledge to make what we feel are important points. But, having "walked the walk" our discussion is also informed by our personal immigrant experiences. Here are some of those experiences:

Acculturation and Identity: A Personal Story
(Joachim O. F. Reimann)

Moving from Germany to the US (San Diego, California) at age 10 in 1960 was an adventure. My friends back home were jealous. After all, America was the land of opportunity and legend. Important things happened in the US which was most commonly depicted by the New York skyline. Most importantly, America was the place where they made very big cars with tailfins.

But the most exposure I had to the English language was a class in the *Realgymnasium*, a German secondary school that prepares students for University entrance. There I learned the word "satchel" and was partly graded by my ability to emulate a very British accent. Needless to say, learning English was a challenge, and the Dr. Seuss books I was presented with at school just didn't cut it. There is just so far that *The Cat in the Hat* or *Yertle the Turtle* could get me.

One of the most memorable pieces of advice was that I should do something about my name. People in the US just couldn't pronounce the "ch" sound in "Joachim." It turns out there is an equivalent in Spanish (Joaquin), but nothing in English. What's worse, by family tradition I have four names – Joachim Oskar Ferdinand Reimann. The two middle names are the given names of my two grandfathers. That was a bit much, even for me.

So, there was a choice to be made. I could be "Akim," or "Joe." But both options came with baggage. Akim is the name of a comic book character in Europe (Google *Akim Held des Dshungels*). As much as I might find comics interesting, that just wasn't something I wanted to be associated with. At the same time, "Joe" was a common name in songs during that period: "Hey Joe, where you goin' with that gun in your hand?" and "Surfer Joe." Given that I was in Southern California, Surfer Joe ultimately beat out the alternative.

As such taking on the name Joe was one of my accommodations to acculturation. At the same time, my identity remained, and remains, very much German. I suspect most people see me as German-American, except people in Germany who just regard me as an American. So, while I still routinely use the name Joe to make things simple for people, my formal documents, including my passport, scientific publications and this book, carry my full and real name, complete with both middle initials. I'm proud to be a US Citizen. But my German heritage also counts.

Did I experience intended discrimination? I doubt it. But I did experience ignorance among my peers and an educational system that was not prepared to respond to my circumstances in effective ways. Early on, fellow students, for example, asked me if I knew Khrushchev (the Soviet Union's leader at the time). This was a perplexing question for me. On later reflection, it appears that, as a German, I must have been seen as one of the bad guys. Many television shows at the time, like *Rat Patrol* & *Combat!* made no effort to distinguish between Nazis and all Germans. Khrushchev was a fellow bad guy and, as such, we presumably all hung out together. Besides, at the end of the 5th grade, the entire class took standardized tests. Having not yet mastered English, I was lost. As a result the classes I was given became remarkably easy until, returning from an open house in the 7th grade, my parents asked me some pointed questions. As highly educated people, they were aghast that their son had been placed in classes for the developmentally delayed (using the term of that time: mentally retarded). My easy time at school was over. I re-took all classes during the summer and finally ended up in advanced courses (including English).

While my process of acculturation involved challenges, it was relatively simple compared to the circumstances faced by non-white, non-European, less well-educated people. For well over 15 years, my clinical practice has included work with people who have fled Somalia and other war-torn areas. Often these refugees have had to deal with the traumatic events they experienced back home, long periods of uncertainty, life in unsanitary and impoverished conditions (like overcrowded refugee camps), fears about the status and safety of people they left behind, and problems adapting to new countries. Not surprisingly some of these displaced persons carry both physical and psychological scars.

The next chapter discusses such factors in more detail.

Acculturation and Ethnic Identity: A Personal Story (Dolores I. Rodríguez-Reimann)

As a psychologist, a regular part of my work involves offering a changed perspective, a context if you will, that gives patients a looking glass to see things differently. That helps compassion, forgiveness, and healing to take place. Therefore, much of the work is psychoeducational. At any one point in time, roughly 45 to 70 percent (45%–70%) of my clinical practice is made up of immigrant patients. Therefore, I will often take the time needed to discuss the meaning of words like "acculturation," "ethnic identity," and "discrimination." This helps patients better understand their own experiences by giving them a language with which to discuss it and view it. Many of my patients have told me that having a "label", a "something to call it," helps them get more of a sense of control over the issues causing them anguish. In that process, I make an effort to point out that experiencing distress is validation that there is nothing "wrong" with them because what they are going through is often difficult and painful. Regularly I hear myself say, "...you know, acculturating—learning the new rules, figuring out who you are, where you come from and who you want to be can be a difficult process". I identify with them, telling them from first-hand experience that experiencing discrimination "really s__ks..."

Concerning my personal experience as an immigrant, let me start backward with my current identity. Who am I and how did I get here? I consider myself a Mexican-American Latina, Ph.D., Clinical Psychologist, wife, daughter, sister, and favorite aunt to my nieces and nephew. I am blessed to be called a friend, colleague, and mentor by many. But most central to my identity, I am a healer with a diverse clinical practice. I am privileged to have people from many different walks of life refer to me as "Doctora" (doctor in Spanish), or "Doc." These are people who trust me to join them in their journeys toward healing and wholeness. Try writing all of that on a name label at a conference! I often tell patients I am "as acculturated as they come." Since I immigrated to the United States when I was an adolescent, I have managed to earn a Ph.D. in Clinical Psychology, two master's degrees (one in Counseling Psychology, one in Clinical Psychology), a bachelor's degree and an associate degree in Liberal Arts.

As an immigrant to this country at fifteen years of age, I had to learn the "new rules" of the game (my short-version description of acculturation). Education and career are areas in my own life which make evident the acculturation process (and choices) I made for my life. I see myself, as what the cultural psychology research literature calls, a Highly Integrated Bicultural, meaning that I can easily navigate between Mexican language /traditions/customs and the larger Anglo society. I refer to myself as Mexican-American, an identity I developed growing up in a small town, called Eagle Pass along the Texas-Mexican border. I also refer to myself as Latina, because I have lived in Southern California for the last 30 years of my life. As an acculturated/bicultural Mexican-American Latina, I mostly watch television and get my daily news in English. But my music choices range from Juan Gabriel and Antonio Aguilar to Madonna, Rod Stewart, and the Celtic Women. Yet, when it comes to familial roles, I have been described by people who are close to me, as "very traditional" in my marriage to my husband of thirty-three years.

Questions to Consider

Our professional work often includes conducting forensic evaluations. These evaluations, which partly rely on psychological testing, are for legal proceedings, including immigration hearings. We use psychological measures—questionnaires—that tell us where people fall along specific psychological dimensions such as depression, anxiety, and perceived discrimination. Imagine a bar chart: the higher the number, the more substantial the experience or symptoms. Where would you fall on that graphic? How much/little emotional distress and discrimination have you personally encountered?

- If you are an immigrant, think about your own experience. How have you navigated through the acculturation process?
- What about your experience with acculturative stress? What has been (or is) particularly stressful about that for you?
- With regards to Ethnic identity-how do you identify yourself?
- What is important to you in that identification process?

Recommendations: Dealing with Discrimination

- Finding healthy ways to deal with discrimination is important for your physical health and your mental well-being. Focus on your strengths. Your core values, beliefs, and strengths can motivate you to succeed and may even buffer some of the negative effects of bias. Overcoming hardship can also make people more resilient and better able to face future challenges.
- Seek support systems. There is strength and comfort in numbers. Family systems are a source of power and wellbeing for many of us. But, as the US civil rights movements have demonstrated over time, groups can successfully push for social and political change, even if it comes slowly. But be

aware that not everyone who claims to be your friend is there to help and support you. If there are efforts to commit violence, dehumanize others, or claim that your group is better than everyone else, walk the other way.

• Don't buy into the negative statements. Some people "internalize" derogatory messages they hear. In other words, they think that, when people repeatedly say something negative about you, it must be true. It is certainly good to be open to constructive criticism and assess yourself accordingly. But negative stereotypes based on racial and ethnic group membership, religious affiliation, national origins, sexual / gender orientation, and other demographics are damaging. They facilitate poverty, hate, violence, housing / job discrimination, and emotional distress.

Acculturation Resources

There are a number of popular books which include stories and anecdotes relevant to acculturation. They don't necessarily use academic language but provide sometimes humorous glimpses into the people's daily cultural lives and experiences. Some are fiction; some are real-world accounts. As a starting point, look at authors such as José Antonio Burciaga, Rudolfo Anaya, Alan Gratz and Nikesh Shukla.

An Organized Way to Move Toward Successful Integration

Later in this book, we discuss our recent work with the Group for Immigrant Integration (GIRA). This presents a model of basic factors that lead to successful integration. Essentially it develops a way of measuring these factors through a measure called the *Successful Immigrant Resettlement Inventory*.

4

PSYCHOSOCIAL FACTORS

Like other populations, immigrants can suffer from a wide variety of psychological disorders including psychoses, emotional disturbances, learning disabilities, substance-related disorders, and other problems. Some immigrants, particularly those undergoing forced migration, have experienced trauma-related psychological disturbances due to war, torture, sexual assault/coercion, discrimination, violence in the form of robbery and theft, and a host of other events. A lack of legal status puts undocumented immigrants at particular risk; they are more often targets because perpetrators expect there will be no repercussions. An August 21, 2018, Washington Examiner report, for example, cited 2,200 deaths, 180,000 rapes, and coerced sex, 81,000 cases of being forced to smuggle drugs, and 27,000 cases of human smuggling during one year.[42] These are just the cases we know about.

In other cases, kidnapped children in war-torn or gang-ridden areas have been recruited to become soldiers or gang members. This has involved drugging kids to decrease their inhibitions around killing, intensive indoctrination, and murdering some children as a warning to others. Such incidents do not show any signs of decreasing. For example, in 2016 alone, UNICEF confirmed 851 worldwide cases involving child soldier recruitment. This was double the number of children recruited the year before. Prominent countries were those in the greater Middle East, Africa, and Central America.[43]

Not surprisingly the long-term effects of violence and conflict on mental health among refugees include high levels of distress. Here is an all–too typical example from our practice:

A middle-aged Somali-origin immigrant is brought in by relatives. This could be a man or a woman. But for purposes of our example, let's say she's a woman. She is very withdrawn and doesn't speak. Her relatives report that she is that way at home as well. They explain that, while living in Somalia right after the regime in power was overthrown during the 1991 civil war, assailants came to the family home. Regime-change left people who had certain clan associations vulnerable to attack and general lawlessness spread throughout the region. The assailants invaded their home, demanded money, killed several relatives, raped some of the women, and hit the lady brought into our office over the head with an AK-47 rifle butt. She lost consciousness for an unclear amount of time. Then the attackers left but threatened to come back. They may have taken family members from the household with them (the remaining family speculated this was what happened but were not entirely certain). In any case, the whereabouts and status of some family members remain unknown.

No significant medical services were available. So, as soon as people in the household recovered enough to travel, they left Somalia and fled to a refugee camp in Kenya. There they encountered barely subsistence-level conditions and suffered extortion demands for money by locals. Fortunately, they did receive very basic medical care. After many years at the camp, they were declared refugees and sent to the US where they did not know the local language (English), customs, or where to go for services.

Given such experiences, it is not surprising that some immigrants suffer from mental disorders and would benefit from treatment. This chapter will explore these issues in the context of fairly common problems, service needs, cultural practices, immigrant concerns about accessing treatment, and ways to overcome such apprehensions. Substance abuse is an additional area of concern. In this process, figuring out what is "cultural," what is psychopathology and what falls under the category of personality traits can be challenging. Later in this chapter we provide a case example of the complexities involved.

Common Psychological Difficulties

Research has shown that migration-related trauma exposure is a significant issue among immigrants. One study, for example, found that 29% of foreign-born adolescents and 34% of the foreign-born parents sampled had experienced trauma in the process of migration. Among those, 9% of adolescents and 21% of their parents exhibited risk for Posttraumatic Stress Disorder (PTSD). Coming from poverty, entering the US illegally, experiencing discrimination in the US, and unsafe living environments all increased that risk. Social support and family closeness decreased it.[44]

Similar patterns have been found in other parts of the world. One German study, for example, found that males with a "migration background" were more likely to suffer from PTSD as well as depression than the local population.[45] Comparable results have been found across multiple other studies in Europe, the US, and other countries.[46]

While immigrants, as a whole, tend to be resourceful and resilient, the process of migration and adaptation can take an emotional toll. This is particularly true among people who have already experienced traumatic events such as assault, persecution and torture in their country of origin. Our research with people from the greater Middle East and East Africa, for example, found that common complaints among adults included helplessness, problems concentrating, nervousness, difficulties expressing feelings, and intrusive thoughts about past trauma. Not surprisingly, those who had experienced persecution in their country of origin plus discrimination in the US described the most numerous and severe difficulties.

Among adolescents, common problems were nervousness, frustration, feeling dejected, and anger. This is consistent with other research. Observations about Syrian refugee children have, for example, shown that continued physical insecurity amplifies and perpetuates distress. Without feelings of stability and security, traumatized children often cannot come to terms with the events they have witnessed. Some studies have estimated the rate of PTSD in such children as high as 76 percent.[47]

Another high-risk group is refugee women and girls. Those who flee their home countries to escape trauma often encounter sexual violence and enslavement. The rape, including the gang rape of women and young girls during war is often a strategy to subjugate, humiliate, and demoralize societies. The message is: submit or this will happen to you or your loved ones as well.[47,48]

Let's clarify how some relevant mental disorders are defined. What exactly is PTSD? What about anxiety and depression? What other things do we need to think about in that context?

Since we have already mentioned PTSD, let's start with that. But we need to say upfront that these descriptions are not meant to be comprehensive. If you feel like you have the symptoms described, don't assume you automatically have the disorder. Rather, go to a professional who can review the difficulties with you.

Posttraumatic Stress Disorder (PTSD)

PTSD is a "trauma and stressor-related disorder" used to describe psychological symptoms that may develop in persons who have directly or indirectly experienced severe emotional or physical difficulties. Examples of possible traumas include combat experiences, serious accidents, work-related injuries, child or elder abuse, rape, assault, political terrorism and persecution, life-threatening illnesses, and natural disasters.[19,20]

As generally described in the literature, PTSD's main features tend to be:

- persistent re-experiencing of the trauma through dreams and waking thoughts,
- emotional numbing or avoidance of experiences and relationships, especially if they are in some way connected to the trauma and,
- symptoms such as anger, anxiety, and/or depression, difficulty sleeping, and cognitive problems such as poor concentration. Persistent and distorted blame of self or others and reckless or destructive behaviors are also fairly common.

It is not surprising that, while "PTSD" did not enter the diagnostic language until around 1980, connections between trauma and psychological disturbances have been historically observed in many cultures. In the past, trauma has been described as *schreckeneurose* (terror neurosis), shell shock, soldier's heat, battle fatigue, and many other labels.[49]

The link between trauma and emotional difficulties has also been recognized across many cultures. While the specific experiences vary,[50] there are commonalities between PTSD and so-called culture-bound syndromes that have been noted.[51] Examples are the Latin American concept of *susto* (generally translated as soul loss or soul fright), and the Cambodian description of *khyâl* attacks (translated as wind attacks).[52]

Anxiety

The American Psychological Association (APA), defines anxiety as "an emotion characterized by feelings of tension, worried thoughts and physical changes like increased blood pressure."[53] Up to a point, anxiety can be helpful. It can make us more watchful for real potential dangers and key up our responses to "fight or flee" so we can survive. But when a person regularly feels anxiety at a level that is not warranted by an immediate situation, it can become a mental disorder. In more extreme circumstances sufferers may experience panic attacks that include increased heart rate, sweating, trouble breathing, and chest pains. These experiences can feel like a heart attack, which further increases the sense of panic.

Anxiety has been described by various labels in different cultures. For example, people from Latin American countries sometimes refer to *Ataque de nervios* ("attack of nerves"). This typically includes symptoms such as intense acute anxiety, anger, grief, trembling, and feelings of heat in the chest.[54]

Depression / Suicide

Throughout our lives, almost everyone feels periods of unhappiness and dejection. But for some people, such difficulties are more long-term and severe and can be classified as depression. This is a mental disorder often characterized by sadness, social isolation, problems sleeping, crying spells, loss of interest in various activities that were pleasurable in the past, decreased physical energy, reduced self-confidence, difficulties focusing and concentrating, as well as a host of other symptoms. In more severe circumstances it can lead to suicidal ideas and even completed suicide. Depression can be caused by environmental stress/personal problems, addiction, biological/genetic factors, serious physical illness, medication side effects, and the aftermath of the pregnancy. Some episodes can be short and transient while others occur over and over again.

Research has shown mixed results when looking at suicide rates among immigrants. Some studies have shown lower rates of suicide attempts among immigrants when compared to the native populations. Others have shown the opposite trend. Immigrants most at risk for suicide attempts appear to be those who are young women of South Asian and black African origin and face language barriers, worrying about family back home, and separation from family.[55] We may not know true suicide rates among immigrant groups because of limitations in the way suicidal behavior is tracked, or not tracked, in various communities.

Substance Abuse

Substance abuse is, unfortunately, a significant problem across the world. As per one United Nations Office of Drugs and Crime report, 264 million people were using illicit substances in 2013.[56] Addiction lends itself to a multitude of medical, psychological and social problems like criminal activity, physical injuries, unprotected sex and the transmission of AIDS and other sexually communicated diseases, motor vehicle accidents, and suicide, not to mention mental and/or physical dependence. Problematic substances include street drugs such as heroin, methamphetamine, cocaine, LSD, and a host of other substances as well as prescribed medications such as opioids and benzodiazepines.

Three million US citizens and 16 million individuals worldwide have had or currently suffer from opioid use disorder (OUD). More than 500,000 in the United States are dependent on heroin. The diagnosis of OUD is made by meeting two or more of the eleven criteria in a year time period.[57]

Personal, social, and financial costs of substance abuse are huge. The US National Institute on Drug Abuse estimated in 2020 that roughly three million people in the US citizens and 16 million individuals worldwide have had or currently suffer from opioid use disorder.[57] In addition more than 500,000 in the US were dependent on heroin. The Centers for Disease Control and Prevention (CDC) has further reported that more than around 81,000 drug overdose deaths occurred in the US over a 12 month period ending in May 2020.[58]

As a result, billions of dollars are spent on health care and law enforcement and are lost in productivity. Similar patterns have been noted in Europe and across the world.

Immigrants and Substance Abuse

As we note throughout this book, immigrants, particularly refugees, often experience great emotional stress and physical trauma. So it is not surprising that some turn to substances as they try to cope with these problems.[59] This can include the substances they know from their country of origin as well as those they learn about in their new home. It is notable that native-born populations are not necessarily familiar with the drugs that are popular (and abused) in other parts of the world.

For example, *khat* or *qat* chewing is common in Ethiopia and across East Africa. This stimulant is a native flowering plant that can cause excitement, loss of appetite, and euphoria. The World Health Organization (WHO) has classified *khat* as a drug of abuse that can produce psychological dependence. While generally illegal in Western countries, this substance is legal in some nations where it has been commonly used (e.g., Djibouti, Kenya, Uganda, Ethiopia, Somalia, and Yemen).[60]

In Syria *captagon* (fenethylline), a synthetic stimulant is popular. A particularly disturbing aspect of both *khat* and *captagon* use is that some rebel groups have been known to use these substances to pump themselves up for battle.

Studies have found that substance abuse disorders tend to be highest among native-born populations and lowest among first-generation immigrants. Second-generation immigrants tend to have higher substance abuse rates than their first-generation counterparts.[61,62] Researchers have seen this as part of the "immigrant paradox" in which new arrivals are healthier because they are more likely to be protected by the cultural norms they grew up within their country of origin (see more information on this phenomenon in Chapter 7).

Statistics suggest, then, that newly arrived immigrants tend to avoid substance abuse while their children are more prone to develop substance-related problems as they adapt to their new country. This, of course, presumes that the new country, as a whole, has greater problems with drugs.

Barriers to Services

Many people with emotional and other psychological problems hesitate to seek care. This can be prompted by social, cultural and religious taboos, fears of being labeled as "crazy", economic restrictions, a lack of information about available services, and poor experiences with healthcare providers. Studies show that Latinos/Latinas for example, experience a host of social and economic obstacles to health care because of limited income and lack of insurance.[63] The American Psychiatric Association (APA) also notes that only 1 in 20 Latinos/Latinas who are in need of mental health seek it, in part due to stigma, discrimination, a lack of knowledge, and for many but not all, a lack of insurance.[64]

Not surprisingly, our research has found that immigrants want providers that treat them with courtesy and respect and explain things in a way they can understand. In addition to financial considerations, problems that limit care include poor treatment by medical staff and front desk staff.[65]

Challenges: Personality Styles and Traits

As in any other defined group, even immigrants from the same country have a lot of within-group diversity. We cannot lump them into one pile and then presume to understand them. They may share some common qualities. But the differences from individual to individual are quite significant. In the last couple of chapters, we discussed psychological processes common to people who share the immigrant experience. The way people navigate this process involves psychosocial factors such as social class, economics, place of origin, education, and so on. Individual differences, such as the degree to which we chose to adhere to the norms of our culture (or not), can also result from differences in the family of origin and individual personality styles.

Suffice to say that, to be effective in working with immigrant populations, healthcare and social service providers must recognize similarities within the immigrant's experience while at the same time knowing how to identify and respect individual differences. This is particularly true when considering individual personality styles and types. For example, some cultures allow for a broader range of emotional expression in mannerisms, volume, and the like. Whether or not eye contact takes place, for example, often depends on gender and age within a cultural group. Recognizing what is acceptable can also significantly differ from culture to culture.

Yet there are also enduring personality styles that can lead to problems no matter who you are or where you come from. This leads us to address personality disorders. Specific diagnoses in this area focus on long-term antisocial, narcissistic, paranoid, hysterical, obsessive, and other problematic traits. These disorders involve problems with a person's long-standing ways of dealing with the world and not just immigration.

Personality Style vs. Personality Disorder in a Cultural Context

When we conduct forensic evaluations with immigrant populations that include psychological testing, we need to take special care in addressing any personality styles that can cause problems for an individual depending on the particular circumstance. For example, a personality that appears to involve "histrionic" (hysterical) tendencies needs to be understood in the cultural context of the individual. What is the culturally acceptable range for emotional expression the person is used to? Is there a norm where being (what much of Western society considers) "loud," is not considered overly dramatic?

Immigrants are often subjected to discrimination because stereotypes towards a particular group may have their origins in the disproportionately publicized behaviors of just a few. These can have lasting consequences for the entire group and can apply to perceptions that the native population has towards immigrants as well as the views immigrants have of the native population.

As we write this book there is much debate about institutional racism in US law enforcement. Some people argue that "a few bad" cops do not represent law enforcement in general. Others say that the volume of abuse perpetrated by the police is in itself evidence of a systemic problem. We suspect that both scenarios might be true. All people have their biases. But there are also people within certain immigrant communities that act in ways that reflect badly on the whole group.

Dolores Rodríguez-Reimann:

Here is an example to make a point. During the "2018–2019 Caravan" migration through Mexico, many of my patients living in Tijuana told me about their perceptions and reactions to the migrants. Some of my patients were sympathetic, and others were not. Yet, I was most intrigued by changes in the perceptions many of my patients reflected towards those in the Caravan as time passed, regardless of what their original opinions were.

I noticed that many had felt initial sympathy for the migrants. However, attitudes grew sour once problems associated with having thousands of people descend on a community began to surface. While "the plan" had been that migrants from the Caravan were "just passing through" Tijuana on their way to the United States, political changes soon led to another reality. Migrants would stay in Tijuana for the "long haul." My patients saw this scenario as a problem. Large numbers of people without resources were coming to "their" city-Tijuana and would undoubtedly create a financial drain to already overwhelmed social service systems. Many of my initially empathetic patients did "not appreciate outsiders" coming to Tijuana. But over time some became impressed with how resourceful and innovative many of the migrants had become in acclimating to their new surroundings. Suddenly they felt respect for "those people." In short, their perception changed again.

Yet with all of the fluctuating opinions, attitudes, and reactions, there was one thing all of my patients seemed to have agreed on. They had strong negative reactions toward a particular migrant who complained about the food she received locally. She was a Honduran single mother who gained social media fame after a local television station interviewed her. In the interview, the lady complained that she and her family were being fed beans and tortillas at a local migrant shelter. She was indignant about such treatment essentially saying that the food was not good enough to give to the pigs back in her home country. Many residents took deep offense, and soon the interview went viral.

Too often, differing cultural nuances or actual individual personality issues give the perception that immigrants feel "entitled" and "not appreciative" when help is offered and given. This seemed to be the case in this instance from what I could understand. According to the story, the lady made it into the United States only to be arrested and later deported after she allegedly committed an assault. One might even consider, at least as reported to me by my patients, "damage had been done to perceptions regarding all immigrants because of just one bad apple that goes viral..."

Did the lady in question have a personality disorder? We can't say because she was not one of our patients. But her attitude did not help her fellow migrants (and ultimately, it appears herself).

Questions to Consider

• Have you struggled with issues of anxiety or depression?
• Have you had to endure trauma? How have you dealt with these issues?
• Do you or did you use substances to cope? Which ones? Does this create a problem for you?
• What has helped you cope?

Recommendations

If you are in emotional distress, do not hesitate to seek professional help. Seek someone familiar with your background. Religious leaders and other people of standing in the community sometimes know of local providers who they like and trust.

5

HEALTH

G ood health is the core ingredient to a happy and successful life. Some immigrants face particular hardships when it comes to caring for their health and well-being. Their physical condition is impacted by the country conditions, diet, and standard care practices in their origins. Also, with immigrants who arrive with little to no material means, there is a question of access to healthcare and information about how acculturation can influence disease prevention and treatment efforts. This chapter explores some of the dynamics involved. This includes traditional healing practices and the impact of dietary changes in a new country. Our discussion is not comprehensive but provides basic examples that, we hope, will spark readers' interest to learn more. As in some other chapters, we then present an individual, in this case, a family story that highlights some of the points we have covered.

In all of this, we need to understand the global context around disease. Viruses and bacteria do not care about international borders. Thus epidemics are expected to become pandemics more frequently in the future. This will require an international understanding of disease transmission and the coordination of resources to combat illness. Here are some factors to consider:

Home Country and Refugee Environments

As in many other areas, issues of health and wellness are fraught with challenges for many who have been forced out of their home country. Syrian refugees, for example, tend to show particularly high rates of respiratory disease. This is probably because they were exposed to chemicals and dust in military attacks back home.[66]

Additionally, a country at war with itself often loses the infrastructure necessary to treat illnesses. For example, Syrian refugee children and youth do not necessarily receive preventive care, such as vaccines, which leaves them vulnerable to diseases like measles and polio. Health problems are further exacerbated by food shortages and thus malnutrition, and a lack of safe housing. This again, makes both children and adults more vulnerable to disease and death.

Such conditions are not necessarily due to a lack skill or dedication among healthcare providers. They are just a byproduct of war. In fact, some circumstances are planned and intended to demoralize and subjugate a population. Within Syria, for example, some parties have specifically targeted hospitals and kill physicians. A 2017 report by the Soufan Center estimates that, at the time, Syrian government forces alone had killed almost 700 medical personnel throughout the country.[47] As per the Physicians for Human Rights group, the rate of such killings had slowed by 2020.[67] But the practice has not stopped entirely.

Home and Host Country Medical Practices

The Syrian example described above is extreme. But even relatively small differences in the healthcare practice between countries can sow confusion. We are, for example, aware that the Bacillus Calmette–Guérin (BCG) vaccine, commonly used outside the US to prevent Tuberculosis, can cause a false positive reaction to a TB skin test.[68] This can create confusion and thus lead to additional and unnecessary diagnostics and treatments.

Immigrants may also face other medical challenges. For example, medications, including non-prescription medications and remedies that people routinely take at home may not exist (or may not be legal) in their new home.

For example, Rohypnol (Flunitrazepam), an especially potent anti-anxiety medication in the family called benzodiazepines (like Xanax and Valium) is used in parts of Europe, Japan, Australia, South Africa, and Latin America. But it is not approved for medical use in the US and has a bad reputation as a street and "date rape" drug.[69]

Diets

People from countries where they have lived on basic (subsistence) diets often have negative physical reactions in countries where fast and other highly processed food is plentiful. It is theorized that their physiology uses food in a way that allows them to store more fat in times where nutrition is more accessible. That allows people to better survive times when food is scarce. But in modern societies food is more abundant, famine is rare, and people just keep growing bigger. This, in turn, puts them at higher risk for type 2 diabetes, heart disease, and a host of other chronic medical illnesses.

Acculturation and Health

Does acculturation impact health? Some research suggests that, in certain areas such as substance abuse and birth outcomes, acculturation is connected with poor adherence to effective health practices. In other areas such as health care access, being more acculturated is likely to yield more positive health outcomes.[70]

Our own research has highlighted some of the complexities involved. For example, we looked at the connections between acculturation, gender, beliefs around health, and people's intent to take actions on such beliefs among Mexican-Americans and tuberculosis prevention. Though we focused on this one aspect of health, it is likely that our results are comparable to acculturation and other disease prevention.

In our research, we used the Health Belief Model (HBM) which considers people's beliefs that a disease is serious, that they are at risk for catching it, what barriers to care they believe exist, and other factors.

Our research found that traditional Mexican-Americans saw tuberculosis as a more serious disease and that they were in more danger of catching than people who were more acculturated. As such, they paid more attention to information on how to prevent tuberculosis than did more acculturated immigrants. This group also said that they were likely to encounter more barriers to good care.

Across the board, women tended to be more health-conscious than men. More acculturated men were least likely to express concern, or act on any concern about tuberculosis among the people we looked at.[71]

It is notable that some theoretical constructs are quite old. The HBM was, for example, originally developed in the 1950s. The fact that it continues in use today speaks to its consistent and ongoing value in understanding people's response to illness.

Traditions and Remedies

Cultural traditions sometimes offer protective factors to immigrant communities. This includes traditional remedies, certain foods, and spiritual and/or religious practices. Too often western medicine dismisses such practices as backward, untested, and unsophisticated.

But that is not always true. Take the example of eating *"nopales"* (or *nopalitos*). These are the pads of the *nopal* (prickly pear cactus plant), a common food in Latino/a culture. Eating *nopales* has traditionally been thought of as helping to regulate blood sugar and therefore as a good diabetes treatment. Studies have shown that there is, in fact, something to that assumption because fiber content in this food helps lower blood sugar levels. Similar results have been found for *karela* (bitter melon) which is commonly used in Asian cultures.[72]

This does not mean that all traditional remedies are useful. For example, the use of mercury in some traditional practices is medically dangerous.[73]

Other common traditional practices include *curanderismo* in Mexico, as well as cupping and coining which has been practiced in East Asia for centuries. Given a lack of clear research-based evidence, some in western medical professions are skeptical about the efficacy of these treatments. Others, like acupuncture, have largely been accepted as helpful because some scientific evidence supports its effectiveness (for example, in helping reduce chronic pain).[74]

Overall, our professional experience has shown that immigrant communities often bring their important healing traditions with them. In addition to Mexican *Curanderos*, the National Institutes of Health (NIH) recognize the importance of Traditional Arabic and Islamic Medicine (TAIM). India's *Ayurvedic* medicine is also considered important among holistic healing practices. It includes the use of indigenous herbs, traditional diets, yogic exercises, massage, meditation, and amulets. Similarly, Traditional Chinese Medicine (TCM) involves complex holistic health and healing practices including the use of local herbs, massage, exercise acupuncture, and healthy, balanced foods. Certainly, most of these more traditional forms of healing can teach us that Western medicine's practice of separating physical, emotional and spiritual healing would benefit from a re-evaluation that considers other forms of healing and a closer look at the advantages of holistic treatment. The Western tradition, which was largely derived from a religious history that separated the body from the mind and spirit, created a disconnection that has not served us particularly well.

An Example from Practice

Occasionally, western providers encounter traditional beliefs in their practice. An example from our practice is as follows:

A Somali client was brought in by her family. Like many of her generation, she had suffered severe PTSD and medical injuries during her home country's civil war. This caused her to experience major problems concentrating which interfered with her ability to learn and remember new information. Consequently she could not pass US citizenship requirements that test for English skills and history/civics knowledge. An exemption to those requirements was eventually granted based on her mental impairment. The client was grateful. She could now get a US passport, use that to go home without problems, and get the services of a traditional healer there who she thought could cure her. The question is: should we have been disconcerted because Western treatment was just a path to the "real" cure or happy that we could help her get to where she needed to go?

> (We chose the latter approach under the auspices of "whatever works.")

Sometimes public health and treatment approaches can be very collaborative. The use of "*Promotoras*" for instance, is a practice of connecting with local community leaders/liaisons and has become a major tool in promoting public health in Latino communities.[75] The practice has proven to significantly impact the same communities with beneficial outcomes. *Promotoras* are also frequently called Community Health Workers (CHWs). They have been an indispensable part of our research projects investigating healthcare needs, not only with Latinos but also with other communities. The success of such programs speaks to the general need for cultural competence in health research and care which Chapter 8 addresses in greater detail.

The Concept of the Healer

One analytical branch of psychology describes archetypes as universal ancient predispositions that have been developed through our collective human history. One such archetype is that of "The Healer." Writer Susanna Barlow[76] tells us that "every culture from the earliest tribes of ancient man, through the ages up to modern times, .. has had within it, the archetype of the Healer." Humans have always had to endure illness. And we have always needed someone to help us heal. Some people appear to have a natural aptitude in that regard. Below is the story of a family member who was one such person. It is included to give one example of how some of the more abstract concepts we have discussed translate into real life.

> **Immigrant Healer (by Dolores I. Rodríguez-Reimann)**
> The life story of Mr. Felipe De Jesus Romo Valadez' often involved healing others. Felipe was born on May

1st, 1903 in La Cruz De Orozco, a small town in the Mexican state of Jalisco, to Mr. Modesto Romo and Ms. M. Santos Valadez de Romo. He was one of his father's nineteen children.

Felipe was raised on a "*hacienda*" (a large land estate, often used for farming or ranching) in Julian Jalisco, Mexico. As the story goes, one of Felipe's favorite chores growing up was to care for the estates' cows. This included bringing them home at night by moonlight.

Modesto, Felipe's father had a local reputation as a healer. He was believed to have a gift that helped cure the sick of neighboring *haciendas*, *pueblos* (small towns or villages), and ranchos (Spanish for ranches). His healing remedies included teas, oils, and prayers. Modesto, a deeply spiritual man, taught these healing methods to Felipe.

Then came the Mexican Revolution which changed the country's political and cultural landscape. It also cost many lives. Among those who died were Modesto and several of Felipe's brothers who fought to defend the Hacienda. Despite these sacrifices, the land was lost, and the remaining family sought a new place where they could start again. In June of 1925, Felipe immigrated to the US, both to find a new life for himself and to help support family members who remained in Mexico.

Felipe and several of his boyhood friends migrated to "*El Norte*" (a common term used by people traveling to the United States from the southern regions of Mexico). They arrived at a US crossing in Laredo, Texas, and paid the 8.00 pesos it took to enter the US at the time. Felipe and his friends had originally planned to go to

Montana. But when they stopped in the small town of Alton, Illinois, they got jobs at the Owens Glass Factory and stayed.

Felipe had originally thought he would return to Mexico within a year. But after three years in Alton, he married Leona Simpkins, the daughter of Charles Simpkins and Delia M. (Ives) Powell. Leona was of German, Cherokee, and French Canadian descent. The couple formed a family and had six sons and four daughters. As was common at the time, these children did not learn Spanish and were largely raised with US cultural norms. Yet they retained a proud Mexican identity.

While some of Felipe's friends returned to Mexico, he remained in the US. This was a frequent experience among Mexican immigrants. They initially thought of their trip to the US as a temporary situation but then they stayed. Some did so because they found new lives. Some felt an ongoing obligation to support family members back home. Yet being an immigrant during the late 1920s–1930s was not easy or safe. Felipe was still treated as "a foreigner," lived in a largely Black and Mexican community called "Dog Town," and, at points reportedly carried a handgun for protection.

As time went on Felipe earned a place of respect in Alton's Mexican community. This was based on his generosity, but also, because of the family gift of healing he had inherited from his father. Felipe's skills included listening to people's stories about "what ailed them," his use of traditional herbs, teas, home remedies, and his prayers. In this process, he earned a reputation for comforting people. Felipe's reputation also helped him mediate community disagreements. People sought his tempered and thoughtful counsel.

Felipe did not visit his beloved Mexico again until 40 years had passed. By then he had raised his children, several of whom served in the US Armed Forces and saw action in World War II as well as Korea and Vietnam. He became a grandfather to many grandchildren and great-grandchildren. Among them, were those who have worked, and continue to work in law enforcement and healthcare. This includes me – Dolores Rodríguez-Reimann - who was and is inspired by my grandfather Felipe's story.

In time, Felipe became ill and his family moved him to Texas. The months that my grandfather Felipe spent in our home were my best memories of him. He passed away in 1983 while living with us, close to Mexico. He suffered two massive heart attacks.

The story of my grandfather Felipe has many aspects of a common immigrant experience. He worked hard, made a life for himself in the US, and served his community. Part of that service involved traditional healing skills that had been passed down to him by his father. Some of his children and grandchildren went on to serve broader society through the military in times of war, through law enforcement, and in many other ways. For me, Felipe passed down a passion for healing. That is part of his legacy.

Questions to Consider

Are there people in your family or community who are known as the go-to persons if you are not feeling well (other than physicians or nurses)?

Recommendations

There are many books on traditional healing. While perhaps not everything will make sense to you, it can be fun to explore how other cultures have seen disease and illness. Some of that may fit your perceptions.

6

CAREER, ECONOMICS, AND EDUCATION

Adjusting to working environments and conditions in a new country can be difficult. It involves challenges on many levels for employers, applicants, and employees. But ultimately, immigrants make substantial contributions to a labor force, including in highly technical occupations. As such they help drive and expand the economies of many countries.

This chapter describes immigrants' basic economic impact, both in terms of the services they need and the contributions they make. We focus on the EU and the US because these locations have been prime destinations for various migrant groups. We also explore barriers immigrants face in accessing a host country's labor market. Additionally, the chapter presents an example of how cultural attitudes toward work can be misinterpreted, to both the immigrants' and the larger society's detriment. Then we present a vignette of the "Reimann story." This is a real-world family account that illustrates career adaptation and success in a new country. Finally, the chapter lists some questions to ask yourself and recommendations you might find helpful.

Migration's Economic Impact

The economic impact of immigration involves a complicated mix of information. On one hand, some immigrants (particularly displaced refugees from less developed countries) will need a range of, and sometimes intensive, social services to get settled. That costs money. Yet immigrants who successfully adjust to their new country can make substantial economic contributions to broader society and to their own sense of safety and happiness. At the same time, immigrants who do not successfully integrate are likely to end up as an underclass that leaves them frustrated, disenfranchised, and disillusioned. In short, a host country that has the political will to make a thoughtful up-front investment in immigrant work transitions will probably reap greater long-term gains.

Here are some relevant statistics. They focus on the EU and the US since, as previously noted, these locations tend to be major (though by far not the only) immigrant destinations. As such they serve as good examples.

The European Union

When addressing the economic costs involved in absorbing immigrants, many countries focus on refugees. This is likely to be the population of most concern since it involves the greatest economic investment. In its review of such issues, a European Commission technical report assessed the available evidence.[77] It acknowledged that too little empirical evidence informs policy debates. But it ultimately concluded that, if done well, the social, economic, and fiscal benefits immigrants bring outweigh more short-term integration costs.

Specifically, the European Commission report studied refugees' impact, and projected impact, on the EU's Gross Domestic Product (GDP). This calculation is the monetary value of all finished goods and services during some defined period. The study considered several different circumstances that might be found over the period starting in 2016 and running through 2040.

While specific scenarios varied, all showed that immigration accounts for, and will continue to account for a notable increase in the EU's GDP. This was true, even when 1) the governmental and societal up-front cost of immigration is considered, and 2) the immigrant group of focus is one that likely needs the most initial help. They concluded that immigration is a net gain for the EU's economy.

The United States

Studies reviewing US employment trends over time show that, among recent arrivals, immigrant men tend to have a smaller chance of becoming employed than their native-born counterparts. But after a period of adjustment, they become even more likely to be employed than the corresponding native-born population. In the beginning, men's occupations tend to be at the lower end of the occupational spectrum meaning they are in jobs that require less education and make less money. But that gap tends to close over time.

Immigrant women have lower initial employment rates than their male counterparts. But their chances of getting a job also increase over time. In terms of wages, they start off making close to what their male counterparts earn. But women then experience comparatively slow growth in salaries. This echoes gender-based wage inequality in the broader population.

To get an overall sense of the dollars and cents involved, consider the following numbers: According to the 2014 National Immigration Forum[78] statistics, immigrants in the United States earned $1.3 trillion in annual wages even then. This amounted to 14.2% of all income earned in the US. Much of this money goes back into the US economy. It thus contributes to the demand for goods, services, and more jobs.

Foreign-born individuals in the US also tend to have more representation in the labor market than other groups. Although they made up 24.1% of the county's overall population, 2016 statistics show they represented 28.8% of its working-age population, 28.4% of its employed labor force, and 30.5% of its workers in science, technology, engineering, or mathematics (STEM) occupations. This trend has had recent times of particular growth. Between 2011 and 2016, for example, the number of working-age immigrants increased by 7.7%, the number of employed immigrants grew to 16.3%, and the number of foreign-born STEM workers rose by 31.5%.

A Closer Look at a Local Impact
In the US, it may also help to look at specific geographic locations to understand immigration's effect at the community level. Some metropolitan areas are, for example, home to immigrants who make up a particularly large percentage of the overall labor market in key industries. These can include agriculture, general services, manufacturing, transportation, warehousing, and construction.

We will use San Diego County (California) as an example. In that locale, immigrants contributed $54.3 billion to the overall GDP in 2016. That amounted to 25.2% of all GDP contributions. These numbers show that immigrants made substantial contributions to the state, local, and federal taxes ($7.5 billion in federal and $2.1 billion in state and local taxes; a $2.4 billion contribution to Social Security and $650.7 million to Medicare).[79]

There may be some assumption that, in part because some immigrants lack legal status, overall immigration constitutes a burden on the US economy. But it has been estimated that, in

2016, such immigrant households earned $2.6 billion. Of that amount, $503.8 million went to federal taxes and $109 million went to state and local taxes leaving the immigrants themselves with $2.0 billion in spending power.[80]

The educational market is another notable economic consideration. For example, 6,965 students were enrolled in San Diego colleges and universities during the fall of 2015 as temporary residents. They went on to support 8,916 local jobs and spend $637.6 million during the 2016/2017 academic year.[80]

Local immigrants also have a role when it comes to housing wealth. In 2016, 43.9% of immigrants in San Diego County owned their own homes. The other 54.1% paid rent. Over fifty-five percent (55.3%) lived in houses. Another 41.1% lived in apartments. The total property value of immigrant households was $79.1 billion and their total annual rent contributions have been estimated at $2.7 billion.[80]

In addition, entrepreneurship plays a substantial part in immigrant contributions. For example, while making up 24.1% of the overall San Diego population, immigrants represented 32.7% of the entrepreneurs in 2016. There were 22.7% more foreign-born than US-born entrepreneurs. These foreign-born individuals generated $1.4 billion in business income for San Diego County. In 2012 for example, Latino/a-owned businesses contributed $11.1 billion in revenue and had 44,950 paid employees. Asian-American owned business generated $10.4 billion in revenue and employed 65,010 people.

The roles played by immigrants also help companies keep some jobs local. One estimate is that by 2016, immigrants living in San Diego County helped create or preserve 36,770 local jobs that would have otherwise moved elsewhere. While exact numbers change over time, the examples cited above illustrate threads that are in all of our best interest and deserve our support and maintenance.

What accounts for such numbers? We believe that immigrants are an enthusiastic and hearty group. As highlighted throughout this book, it takes a lot to pack up and leave the place you know, the place you've called home. Some people don't have a choice. To stay might mean poverty, violence, or even death. Others feel that they could be/do more with their lives than their original country was able to foster. In some cases, immigration allows the top minds in a particular field to collaborate in one place and come up with discoveries that benefit humanity as a whole. Our message in talking to immigrants is as follows: whatever your circumstance is, don't give up. You have already proven that you are strong. Migration has been a form of advancement as long as there have been people. Use that strength to forge ahead, not only for yourself but for your family's future.

Assessing all of the above, it is clear that, rather than being a drain on host country resources, immigrants make substantial contributions to many labor markets and the economic health of society as a whole in their adopted country.

Barriers to Success

Despite the positive numbers described above, challenges remain. Using 2017 figures, for example, the National Academies of Sciences, Engineering, and Medicine concluded that foreign-born workers are overrepresented in high-level professional groups that require the most education (e.g., scientists, engineers, and architects).[81] In other words, they make up a higher percentage of workers in such fields than the native-born population. But, at the same time, foreign-born workers are under-represented in other professional and management positions.

The US Bureau of Labor Statistics reports that, on average, foreign-born persons earned only 83.1 % of the income made by their native-born counterparts in 2016.[82] If you are recruited by a company based on your professional skills, or you have money to invest, this is generally not a problem. You may well have significant opportunities.

But this option is not always viable for immigrants, even if they have a substantial education. For example, in one project we conducted with persons of Middle Eastern and East African origins in San Diego (Project *Salaam*) we found that most people had a High School Diploma or greater educational level. Yet the group was also clustered at the lower end of the economic spectrum (most making less than $2,000 per month). Bar charts from the project reflecting this reality are presented below.

Highest formal grade or year of school

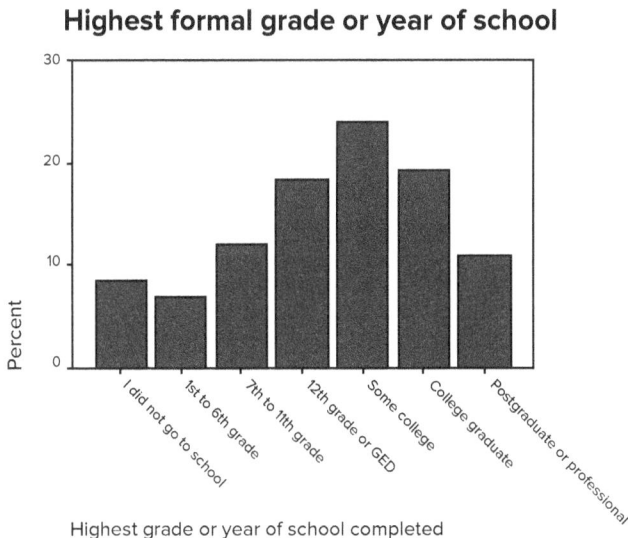

Monthly Income

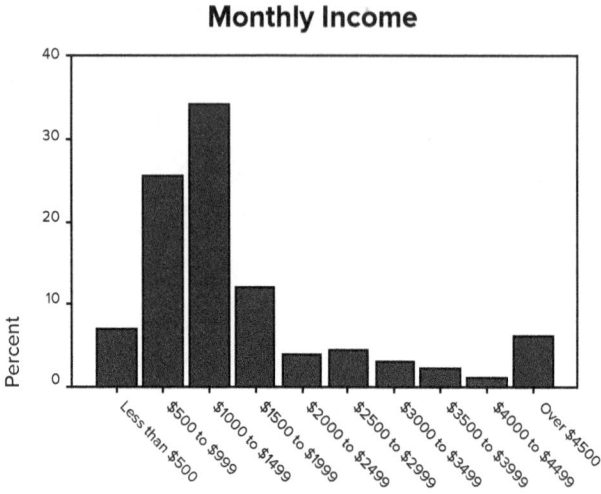

Barriers included the fact that host counties tend not to accept some foreign credentials. This is particularly true in the healthcare professions.

We, for example, have a friend who received her medical degree in a foreign country. This was not an MD earned at some mom-and-pop marginally accredited offshore medical school. Rather, it was earned from a generally respected institution. Our friend was (and is) quite competent, having held several positions of responsibility in other parts of the world. But since the qualifications were not accepted in the US, she had to get a second medical degree here so that she could practice her chosen profession.

Not everyone is willing or able to take such a large step backward. Not everyone has the million-dollar plus investment required to essentially buy into new countries. We have highly educated and capable people working in low-level occupations.

That type of experience involves changes in socioeconomic and social status which can be quite jarring for them.

Social and Political Considerations

Another consideration for immigrants, even if they are moving as part of a company recruited or for high-level positions, is the legal, social, and political climate in their new country. In 2019 we attended an international conference by an association of immigration attorneys from many places across the world. One panel of legal experts addressed the degree to which LGBTQ+ people are perceived in various countries. Panel members' responses ranged from 1) we recognize the circumstances involved and have laws that protect civil rights; to 2) in our country we know the issues involved but need to do more in terms of laws that protect human rights, to 3) one attorney's reply (paraphrasing): same-sex relationships are a crime in my country.

This type of circumstance is just one example of a broader question about the social and political climate in countries people migrate to. Are people fairly open-minded regarding the lifestyle and values you espouse? Are there laws that protect human rights? If so, are those laws enforced? How do these factors compare to realities in your country of origin? The answers can have an obvious impact on your social as well as work-life and wellbeing.

Vocational and Career Choices Across Cultures

Other questions include: How do people from other cultures decide on career paths? Do these approaches match common employer expectations in their new country?

One of our studies explored such issues.[83] It looked at factors that influence young adult Mexican-Americans' career decisions. Demographic data at the time showed that this group had more difficulties accessing the labor market than the broader population. Research further suggested that this trend was partly driven by employers' misconceptions. Specifically, some employers perceived Mexican American young adults as lacking focused career goals, aspirations, and paths. Such presumed lack of focus was interpreted as a type of vocational immaturity (limited commitment to a specific occupation) and thus as a detriment. The career development literature has used pathological and critical-sounding terms such as "zeteophobia" (a presumed fear of making career decisions) and "career promiscuity" to describe people who do not have a highly specific career track in mind.[84] Besides, there was the presumption that limited career goals meant a person was more focused on family and thus as less ambitious.

Our study, however, found that young adult Mexican-Americans who were willing to accept a greater range of career options particularly valued community cohesiveness and a strong work ethic. What was regarded as a lack of career goal clarity was a kind of flexibility, arising, in part, out of a desire to accommodate and respect other people's needs. Rather than being indecisive and unfocused, those Mexican-Americans who expressed career flexibility often did so to fit themselves into the requirements of an organization. To them, such flexibility signified a willingness to work hard to succeed. In this context, the pursuit of a narrowly defined career goal, associated with self-interest and an inward focus, was less important. Our results also showed that neither men nor women who placed a strong focus on their families showed any related decrease in work ethic. Instead, for most Mexican-Americans, feeling discriminated against rather than involvement in the family hurt their career investment.

One might think that a person's socioeconomic status has an impact on such results. In other words, a person who is poor is more likely to "take anything" in terms of employment. While that may be true in some circumstances, such a trend was not evident in our study.

In summary, this research highlights that, while a focus on family plays a part in Mexican-Americans' workplace decisions, this focus does not limit contributions to the workplace. If anything, it may enhance employees' value.

Unfortunately, most employers have not adjusted their staff selection process to this type of reality. Vocational and career experts have, for example, deemed "transferable skills" and "cross training" as an important area of focus for years. The term means that work skills acquired in and for one type of occupation can also be useful in another one. We just have to figure out which skills go with which occupations. But it is difficult finding such considerations on any job announcement.

At the same time, it is increasingly important to consider the impact of culture on career choice. If employers and career development professionals do not do so, they 1) reduce the number of good employees they hire and 2) are not adapting to workforce trends which no longer fit a "one life/one career" model and is, instead, moving to a more fluid and flexible reality.

> **Bernhard Erwin Ferdinand Reimann, Dr. rer. nat.**
> **A father's story by Joachim Reimann**
> A real-life example from our family illustrates some of the circumstances raised above. In 1960 my father, Dr. Bernhard Reimann, was recruited by a San Diego-based

research institute to set up that facility's first electron microscope. He was a biologist by training and a second-generation expert in using such advanced instruments. In this case, the microscope was manufactured by the German company Siemens. My father had been trained in Berlin, a center of development for that technology at the time.

The original assignment was for one year. But, at the time, someone who had left the European academic system had severe difficulties getting back in. There were also research grants to be had in the US, and who would not want to stay here? Like most immigrants, my father encountered challenges. These included learning English and living in an unfamiliar environment. Additionally, in 1960 the end of World War II was only 15 years distant. There was still a popular assumption that all Germans had automatically been (and still were) "Nazis." While untrue, this perception often made professional and social interactions unnecessarily awkward and stressful.

Once my father had become established, the rest of the family followed. We have been here ever since. Ultimately my father had a long career working as a civilian for a US Department of the Army medical facility. There he was one of the first people to use an electron microscope as a diagnostic tool for cancer and other illnesses, which allowed for better medical treatment of military service members and their families. Toward the end of his time in civil service, my father received the Army Commander's Award for Civilian Service Medal. This award is given to US Army employees who have established a sustained pattern of excellence. My father also made over 70 contributions to scientific literature, most of which appeared in peer-reviewed research journals. In his retirement, he wrote three books largely based on his experiences as a child, adolescent, and young adult in Germany. Even in retirement he continued to be active and engaged in other productive ways. Living in a small village in New Mexico, he helped develop a 911 emergency call system there. He also came up with an ecology-friendly water purification system which was important in a place where water is a scarce resource.

This story illustrates several points. Certainly, there were challenges to be overcome, though our family's migration was easier than many others'. But my father's story reflects the benefits migration can bring, both for the person coming to a new country and for that country itself. We arguably had a better life than we would have had otherwise. But my father also brought expertise that was lacking in the US at the time. He then used that knowledge to further benefit science and medicine working on the vanguard of new medical diagnostics. His assets to his adoptive country didn't end in retirement. He used his expertise to help the community where he lived.

Questions

If you are an immigrant who is looking for employment in your new country, or you are someone who helps immigrants in that process, it may make sense to develop an employability plan. Common questions in such a plan are as follows:

- What kind of work do I like to do?

- What skills and experience do I have?
- What kind of schooling do I need to be hired?
- How can I show potential employers that I would be good at a job?

Measurement

Most people would want to work in a job they enjoy and one that fits their personality. Being engaged intellectually, mentally and even spiritually on the job is a motivating factor for success. Fulfilling work means less absenteeism due to stress and illness and a sense that the paycheck isn't all that matters. Several systems can help identify general areas where people might like to work, and the specific work involved. Interest inventories systematically identify occupations that have a certain characteristic in common. Work with machines could, for example, translate into a variety of occupations in engineering and mechanics. Artistic interests fit many areas such as music, painting, and cinema. Inventories that make the connection between what you like and various specific occupations include the Strong Interest Inventory (one of the most well-known measures), O*NET Interest Profiler, the CareerZone Interest Profiler, and the Student Interest Survey for Career Clusters. Some are available online (e.g., the MnCareers Interest Assessment). For people who have trouble reading, there is the Pictorial Interest Inventory and the Picture Interest Career Survey. Several of these inventories are free.

Some of these measures are also available in multiple languages including German, Arabic, and Spanish (e.g., the Personal Globe Inventory, the Career Interest Inventory).[85]

Resources

Let's say you have identified a general category of occupations that fits your interests and personality. Now you want to explore various occupations that fall under your category. One probably under-utilized resource to learn about occupations in the US is the Department of Labor's Occupational Outlook Handbook. It gives you a wealth of information about educational and other requirements needed to enter a profession, what people in the profession do, average compensation at various points of a person's career for that profession, and to what degree there is a need for the occupation in the future.

The Handbook can be found online at https://www.bls.gov/ooh/.

Resources in other nations also track occupational outlook data. Such resources include the Job Market Monitor in the UK, the German Center for the Development of Vocational Training, and the Organization for Economic Co-operation and Development (OECD) (data for 37 countries).

.

7

RESILIENCE & EMOTIONAL INTELLIGENCE

As described throughout this book, immigrants face a number of stressful situations as they undertake the journey to a new country and then settle in that country. Available evidence shows that many do better than their counterparts who remain at home. Paradoxically some also do better than their second-generation off-springs.[61,86] Others do not do as well.

This begs the questions: What qualities cause some people to adapt better than others? Why do some people who have been exposed to traumatic circumstances have severe and long-lasting emotional reactions while others do not? Answering such questions may help us find ways to foster success. This chapter explores such issues by discussing individual qualities and cultural factors.

Psychological resilience has been defined as the mental and emotional ability to deal with a crisis. Even if there is an initial negative reaction, resilience helps us recover more quickly from traumatic events. Resilience is the ability to protect oneself from the negative effects of stress. In short, resilient people are more able to remain calm during a crisis, act effectively to counter it. Not surprisingly, immigrants with greater resilience levels are more immune against trauma related distress.[87]

As described throughout this book, immigrants can face a multitude of challenges and stressors in their adopted country. These include discrimination based on the larger society's negative stereotypes and misconceptions.[88,89]

A detailed analysis of actual facts about immigration debunks such stereotypes. Despite that, the myths endure. Having the psychological strength to counter negative perceptions and endure despite naysayers is critical to emotional welfare and success.

Research has shown that some adherence to home-country cultural beliefs can protect people against problems. The literature has, for example, described a "Latino paradox" or "Hispanic paradox." Simply put, this phenomenon refers to research showing that first-generation Latino Americans tend to have health outcomes that are roughly equivalent to (or sometimes better than) their "Anglo" counterparts.[90] This is considered a paradox because first-generation Latinos tend to have lower average income and education, factors that are generally connected with worse health and higher mortality rates across the world. While such observations were initially connected with physical health (e.g., obesity and diabetes) further research has observed similar trends in psychological well-being.

Although this scenario appears to be particularly true of first generation immigrant populations it becomes less pronounced in later generations. Second-generation Latinos have, for example, shown greater risk than their first-generation counterparts for depression, anxiety, suicidal ideation, behavior disorders, conduct and eating disorders, and substance abuse.[61,63] Similar patterns have been identified for populations emigrating from Asia and the Caribbean.

The existence of this phenomenon has been challenged by some, based on limitations in the research (e.g., statistical biases) that was used to identify it.[91] Regardless, it has been observed in many instances that such critiques carry limited weight.

What accounts for this phenomenon? In part, it may be that people who are willing to undertake (and who survive) a migration tend to be healthier and psychologically more robust and persistent than those who remain at home. In addition, first-generation migrants may be more likely to stick to traditional beliefs that are familiar and thus soothing, cultural admonitions against substance abuse, as well as dietary practices that their bodies are most accustomed to. In addition, there may be strong traditions around family solidarity and interconnections which result in a strong support system.

Subsequent generations are then more likely to adopt higher-risk practices including drug abuse and dietary changes (e.g., "supersized" meals in a fast food culture). In addition, they may be more cognizant of and thus stressed by their minority status, consequent biases, and societal barriers that potentially limit their success. Thus the optimism which drove first-generation migration is likely to erode among second generation immigrants. In short, hanging on to some family traditions and traditional diets (though not the fast food version of such diets) may be both physically and psychologically healthy.[90]

Another concept to consider in learning who adapts better has been termed "emotional intelligence." This is the capacity to be aware of, control, and express one's emotions effectively. Such ability increases the chance that we will be able to handle interpersonal relationships thoughtfully and with empathy. Emotional intelligence is often thought to have five basic components: self-awareness, self-regulation, internal motivation, empathy, and social skills.[92]

Essentially self-awareness is the ability to understand our own emotions, strengths, weaknesses, drives, values and goals. In addition we then have to recognize how our expressions in these arenas impact other people. Self-regulation is how well we control any negative disruptive emotions and impulses. We also have to consider how well we adapt to changing circumstances (certainly a major factor for immigrants). Social skills involve our ability to get along with others. Empathy is how well we consider other people's feelings as we make decisions. In that context "motivation" is our awareness of what drives other people.

If we are able to understand, balance, and apply these factors, we are likely to be more confident, more effective with others, and less stressed. It also has the potential to help you lead others.

How do you gain emotional intelligence? Providing a full course on the subject is beyond the scope of this book. But, in a nutshell, it requires an honest assessment of how you do things now and if those current methods work. If they don't, consider changing your habits and methods. If you get negative reactions from others try to put yourself in their place so you can find empathy for, and identification with them. In addition, consider how you respond to adversity. If you become upset, does that solve the problem? How we act is something we have in our control. But there are things that are clearly not in our control (e.g., some other people's actions). Take responsibility for your own actions. If necessary, make apologies and correct mistakes. It's important to know that resilience is not given to you by your genetic makeup. It involves qualities and skills that can be learned with care and practice.

What does resilience look like in real life? Here is an example from our clinical practice: A husband and wife came to our office. They had eight children. Both adult parents were Somali refugees and had no formal education whatsoever. The wife was severely impaired by PTSD, The husband worked hard at menial jobs to make ends meet, never giving up on the promise of a better life in the US. That, in and of itself, deserved a lot of respect. But probably the most amazing family accomplishment was that eventually all eight of their children were either attending a top 25% university or (for the younger children) were enrolled in advanced high school programs. In one generation the family had gone from literally zero formal schooling to top-level educational achievement.

Several ways in which family members thought about, and approached their lives accounts for this success. The mother was severely disabled. But the father and children were psychologically robust. The father, in particular, was able to understand difficult life circumstances in constructive ways. One example illustrates the point: Upon gaining US Citizenship the father traveled to Kenya and met with a brother he had not seen in many years. They talked at length about their lives and the love they shared for their family. The brother died the very next night. While saddened by this sudden and unexpected event, the father expressed gratitude for his chance to have met the brother one last time. He interpreted it as fate, a gift from God. In other words, he found a way of looking at the situation that was positive.

Family members also relied on their own abilities to succeed in the US. While accepting aid as needed, they did not expect broader US society to care for them indefinitely. Rather, they used their own persistence, creativity, adaptability, and hard work to succeed.

Questions to Ask Yourself

Here are some statements you can think about when you consider resilience and emotional intelligence. Are these statements true for you or not?

- I can depend on my family and friends.
- I know I will succeed in life even if it is difficult.
- I seek advice or help from others at times when I need it.
- I apologize when appropriate.
- I speak when spoken to and tend to smile when others smile at me.
- I can express differences of opinion, criticism, or complaint without antagonizing others.
- I can be relied upon to do what I say I will do.
- I make positive statements about myself and demonstrate positive concepts.
- I get along with others in group interactions.
- I accept constructive criticism without becoming angry.
- I understand how to avoid trouble with police or other authorities.
- I can verbalize a realistic understanding about ways of coping with situations.

- I actively engage in problem-solving behavior.
- I complement and encourage others.
- I help others even without consideration of personal gain.
- I make my own opinions and preferences known.
- I take part in social events and get involved in group functions and activities.
- I actively engage in problem-solving behavior related to personal, family, or social problems.
- I appraise my own abilities and accomplishments realistically.
- I make realistic goals for myself.
- I believe I am good at a lot of things.

8

CULTURAL COMPETENCE

Cultural competence is the ability to recognize social and cultural lenses through which immigrants understand and act in their daily lives. Such competence helps countries and communities work with immigrants.

Cultural competence is a complex and broad topic that really deserves its own book. It is relevant to a variety of areas including issues around diversity and inclusion in companies, government, other organizations, international business and trade, legal decision-making, global health, and any circumstance in which people from various national and cultural backgrounds interact. In this chapter we provide a basic overview of the topic as well as some relevant examples from our own experience. These examples include research efforts aimed at structural policy improvements like how to best license healthcare providers and ways to enhance services at a community level. In addition, we provide a case example of how culture can play itself out in the clinical setting. We hope that our comments will whet your appetite to further explore this important arena.

The US Office of Minority Health defines cultural competence as "*having the capacity to function effectively as an individual and an organization within the context of cultural beliefs, behaviors, and needs presented by consumers and their communities.*"[93] We add that cultural competence is a skill that must be learned. As such it is not automatically granted or denied by your racial, ethnic, cultural, national, or other group membership. In addition, being "competent" does not mean you are an expert (or speak for) some particular cultural group. It just means you have enough awareness and skill to be reasonably effective. It is one step in a process that begins with ignorance of other cultures and moves to proficiency in understanding and working with people from other cultures.

Most basically, cultural competence includes three dimensions: 1) cultural knowledge about a particular group, 2) awareness of the attitudes and beliefs you have towards people who are from a different culture than your own, and 3) skills in the use of culturally appropriate rapport building, assessments and interventions. In the helping professions, this includes attention to and promoting culturally effective treatment practices and access to a variety of services (e.g., qualified interpreters or legal experts).[88]

According to the American Psychological Association's (APA) mission statement, cultural competence should be an inherent principle that underlies all services performed by psychologists. In part, this premise applies to individuals from culturally and/or linguistically distinct ethnic and racial groups and specifically includes immigrants.[88]

So, what does cultural competence entail? Many people from culturally and linguistically distinct groups have had poor experiences with healthcare and social service providers. Such reactions have been prompted by negative encounters ranging from basic insensitivity to major human rights abuses.[94] This has led to distrust of medical advice such as taking the COVID-19 vaccine.[95] In addition, cultural taboos limit some people's willingness to participate in assessment and treatment efforts. To change that, building rapport and respect are critical.

While it may be counterintuitive, the road to cultural competence begins with self-understanding rather than outreach to people from other groups. Too often, well-meaning people can have biases towards, and preconceived notions about those who are different even when such biases are unintentional and at odds with how we view ourselves. But this is not an insurmountable problem. If you accept the reality that we all have some biases, you have taken the first and arguably most crucial step towards cultural competence.[88]

A study of physicians we published a while back illustrates the point. The basic information it yielded is still relevant today. Our results found that simple exposure to ethnic groups in clinical practice did not, in and of itself, facilitate culturally competent care. Rather such care was most directly prompted by 1) our ability to recognize that cultural factors are an important consideration in healthcare and 2) awareness that personal biases around cultural groups can keep us from providing the most effective professional services.[96]

Accepting that all of us have biases, no matter how unintentional, is difficult. One common reaction may be "*...not me, I don't do that...*" But without acknowledging our own preconceptions, our efforts to understand various communities can become an exercise in what we have sometimes termed "*viewing cultures on parade*" in our cultural competence training. In other words, we experience a specific group's traditional foods, music, dress, and customs from the sidelines and then judge them through our own background. In contrast, recognizing our own biases helps us suspend this inclination and strive to understand a community's customs from its own point of view.[97]

It is important to note that cultural competence does not require us to automatically accept all behaviors people claim as traditional. Basic social justice is an important consideration. Simply put, no cultural, religious, or other claims excuse violence against or subjugating others. However, being mindful of our own potential biases does help us to separate the functional from the dysfunctional within our own as well as in other cultures.

Having reviewed some fundamentals, we can now discuss a few considerations in the cultural competence framework. Here are just a few things we have had to think about:

Language & Interpretive Services: Who provides these services? Are we using professional interpreters or family members? Do the professional interpreters know the regional dialects of the people we work with? Sometimes adult relatives are the most viable option. But using children or adolescents in the role of the interpreter is never a good idea. Such considerations are important in healthcare, legal cases involving immigrants, government-based services, and in many other settings.

Dietary Practices: Have people undergone dietary changes with acculturation which have resulted, or can potentially result in health problems (e.g., obesity, type 2 diabetes?)

How Problems are Described: In some cases, psychological symptoms are described in physical terms since that is how they are perceived and more socially acceptable. (It's better to be sick than crazy.)

Consider Body Language: For example, practices around eye contact and handshakes vary across cultural and religious practices.

Family Dynamics & Social Rituals: Family roles can change with immigration and acculturation depending on the financial earners or the family members who have learned the new language most quickly. Often, the children in the family then step in to help adults understand locals. This is, however, problematic in healthcare, social service, economic, legal, and other discussions where information that should not be shared with children is addressed.

Socioeconomic Status: Similar to family dynamics, socioeconomic status can change with migration. Suddenly the former doctor or attorney in the native country is driving a cab in the new country. Even if it's temporary, such role reversals can take some adjustment.

Gender: Having a physician or other provider that matches a patient's gender may be a priority, especially in the case of physical examinations. This is often true regardless of culture but may involve special religious or social taboos in some circumstances. It is also important to have providers who are experts in issues around gender identity involved in cases where that is a concern. In addition, knowing who tends to be the healthcare advocate (for example, who prompts spouses and children to get care) in various cultures is important.

Letting People Know about Services: How do providers let people know about available services? What methods work best when we attempt to inform a community through outreach and education? Letting people know that services are usually confidential, and the legal limits of such confidentiality are important factors. Obviously having staff members who speak the community's language is critical.

What Diagnostic & Treatment Methods Apply? For healthcare and particularly mental health practitioners it's important for you to know that the assessment tests you use are valid for people from different cultural backgrounds. This includes using the right language. But it also requires us to know how different cultures understand health and illness.

What happens in cases where cultural competence was not practiced? Here are just two real examples we are aware of:

1. One of our clients applied for social services based on a mental disorder. She was denied assistance because she dressed in bright colors for one meeting where eligibility was determined. The assumption was that people who are depressed would wear bland clothing that reflects their bleak mood. The lady was of Somali origins where brightly-colored dresses are the norm. She had also been dressed by relatives for such an important appointment.

2. Another client told us of missing an appointment with a new physician. Asked why that happened she responded that she showed up on time but was given English language documentation to complete before the doctor could see her. While this client spoke some English, she was not literate. There was no one in the waiting area that could help her, and the front office staff appeared to be busy. Consequently, the client went outside to look for someone who could assist her. By the time she returned to the doctor's office, it was too late for her to be seen. This type of scenario is not limited to healthcare. Problems with language and literacy also occur in business, government, legal, financial, and many other circumstances.

As demonstrated by these two examples, achieving cultural competence, let alone cultural expertise, is important and requires us to address many elements. To help both individuals and organizations, the United States Office of Minority Health developed the National Standards for Culturally and Linguistically Appropriate Services in Health and Health Care (aka the CLAS Standards). These standards provide a framework that improves health care quality and advances health equity within organizations that serve increasingly diverse communities in the US. The overriding principle is to "provide effective, equitable, understandable and respectful quality care and services that are responsive to diverse cultural health beliefs and practices, preferred languages, health literacy, and other communication needs."[98]

Internationally, research and advocacy around cultural competence have also emphasized the importance of global health. In other words, we need to understand health and illness in the context of populations that migrate, climate change, worldwide economic relationships that facilitate travel, and other factors. This perspective puts emphasis on interdisciplinary approaches that join epidemiological, cultural, financial, environmental, ethnic, political, and legal contexts. While highly ambitious, it recognizes that we live in an interconnected world in which health and wellness are worldwide rather than country-by-country issues.[99]

Over the years, in addition to our clinical psychology practice and public health research, we, the authors, have conducted training in Cultural Competence. While these have often been in healthcare, they have also involved attorneys, employers, governmental agencies, housing service providers and other settings. Over the years we have also conducted a number of community assessments that identified the specific needs of immigrant groups and remote locations within the US. These efforts were conducted to mitigate health disparities. We wanted to help groups of people, particularly immigrants, who have systematically experienced greater obstacles to healthcare and other services due to a multitude of circumstances. These included their racial or ethnic group membership national origins, religions, socioeconomic status, gender, age, mental health, disabilities, sexual orientation or gender identity, geographic location, and other characteristics that tend to get in the way of adequate services.[100]

Next, we will describe three of projects we developed and carried out in order to highlight how some of the concepts addressed above play out in the lives of individuals who face specific needs and circumstances. We describe these projects and then summarize the most relevant points that service providers, policy experts, administrators, lawmakers, community developers, and the immigrants themselves can take away from them.

Project *Salaam*[101] was basically a psychological and general health needs assessment that focused on members of the greater San Diego's Middle Eastern, North African, and East African communities. It was a joint effort including people from a variety of backgrounds. Organizationally, it involved a partnership between an academic institution - San Diego State University's Graduate School of Public Health – and a faith-based institution, the Islamic Center of San Diego (ICSD). The project incorporated experiences of individual team members who were licensed mental health clinicians, medical care providers (some had done so in multiple countries), and others who had knowledge pertinent to these communities. In short, the project combined and integrated the expertise of academics, health service workers, and people who were embedded in the communities we wanted to help.

Project *Salaam* was developed because, in the early 2000s, those of us who practiced clinical psychology became increasingly aware of emotional distress among members of San Diego's Middle Eastern, North African, and East African communities. Individual clients described negative experiences and how they were trying to cope with such experiences in their day-to-day lives. Among immigrants, a history of adverse experiences included persecution, imprisonment, and torture in their country of origin. These clients also described experiencing harassment and discrimination in the US. They further told us that such incidents had escalated in response to the terrorist attacks of September 11, 2001 in New York, subsequent terrorist attacks in various parts of the world, and US military actions in Iraq and Afghanistan.

Some of our key findings were as follows: A substantial number of San Diego's immigrants from Middle Eastern, North African, and East African regions experienced persecution in their countries of origin. In addition, members of these backgrounds that had migrated to San Diego reported notable levels of harassment, discrimination, and hate crimes. They tended to say that harassment was based on their religious beliefs, the way they looked and dressed, and their cultural ethnic group membership. For Arabs and Muslims, the traditional dress was reported as most frequently why they felt targeted. Members from other groups including Chaldean Christians were not exempt. (Chaldeans are part of the Catholic Church and have their origins in Middle East, mainly in north Iraq, southeast Turkey and northeast Syria.) Specific experiences ranged from subtle forms of discrimination to violent confrontations. Adolescents and children reported notable levels of bullying and harassment, often in their schools from classmates. Children also reported stereotyped and hurtful comments made by their teachers. Only a small proportion of those who experienced harassment and discrimination reported it to anyone. Common reasons for the decision not to report were not knowing who to report to, the belief that reporting it would be ineffective, and a desire not to draw attention to themselves. In fact, among adults who reported adverse experiences, only 12% were satisfied with the outcome.

Among immigrants, those who experienced persecution in their countries of origin reported more trauma-related psychological difficulties than those with no such experiences. Those with trauma experiences both in their country of origin and in the US reported more psychological difficulties than any others in the groups. Overall problems described most often by adults were difficulties expressing feelings, problems working, feeling helpless, difficulty concentrating, nervousness, and feeling detached from others.

Experiences of persecution in a persons' home country were particularly linked with thoughts of death and difficulties expressing feelings. Those who'd experienced torture most often cited detachment from others and anger toward self. Harassment in the US was particularly linked with anger, loneliness, feelings of guilt, and marital problems. Difficulties working and increased family discord were also described among the group. This included some reports of domestic violence and divorce.

Youths often described their parents as unavailable to talk to about their problems. Both adolescents and adults acknowledged increased communication and emotional gaps between parents and their children. Those with strong religious conviction attempted to cope with stress primarily through prayer.

But many also acknowledged that this was only a partial solution. Others reportedly denied any difficulties because they saw stress as a personal weakness and feared being considered "crazy." Members of Middle Eastern, North African, and East African communities in San Diego often saw formal mental health services as unavailable to them. In part, this was caused by a lack of culturally and linguistically competent providers. In addition, the cultural stigma associated with emotional problems made people reluctant to seek care. Like other immigrant groups, first-generation immigrants from the Middle East, North Africa, and East Africa had less access to health insurance than people in the broader US population. This problem extended to their children and adolescents, and particularly to those with limited or no English skills. These same people also described greater difficulties finding a doctor and making medical appointments. Finally, 60% of our survey respondents said they had stopped visiting a particular doctor, clinic, or hospital because of the poor treatment they had received.

Project *Salaam's* outcome was that, as a written report, we were able to distribute information about the needs of a largely immigrant group of people whose circumstances had been poorly understood. We also made key recommendations that described how this community could be assisted. Finally, we had a large meeting with community members and law enforcement dealing with hate crimes in which we shared our findings. This allowed participants to know that they had been heard by us and gave them the opportunity to give us additional feedback.

Project *Salud Libre*[102] was an assessment of mental health needs among the mostly rural and largely immigrant Mexican-American communities in California's Imperial Valley. The assessment was performed by a local community clinic system with major support and consultation from us.

Our assessment was prompted by the community clinic's knowledge of its rural surroundings. Best national data show that people living in such settings experience significant health care access barriers. They often have lower family incomes and are less likely to be covered by health insurance than their urban counterparts. In addition, fewer skilled providers are available in rural setting than in their urban counterparts. Latinos face the potential double jeopardy of regional and ethnic-specific service deficits.

These circumstances are true for mental as well as physical healthcare. Nationally, limited mental health services for rural and culturally distinct populations have been cited as causing several problems. Fewer people obtain any care at all. Those who do get help tend to do so later in the course of their illness. Consequences include more severe, persistent, and disabling symptoms that are more expensive to treat than would have been the case with early intervention.

The *Salud Libre* assessment consisted of data gathered through surveys, structured focus groups, and key stakeholder interviews. Activities were conducted in Spanish and English across many locations spanning Imperial County. The surveys compiled demographic, acculturation, mental health symptom, service access and utilization, care preference, and related information.

The recognition that Imperial Valley residents tend to experience significant stressors was one of the key findings. These stressors included unstable economics, extreme summer heat, isolation, and physical illness. Most commonly cited mental health symptoms were related to anxiety, depression, and frustration. In addition, people often described physical difficulties that they tended to connect with emotional problems. Women, adolescents, the elderly, those who were less acculturated, and those who spoke little to no English appeared to be at most risk for emotional distress. Stressors and mental health symptoms caused and exacerbated impairments in activities of daily living in school and family settings. Family discord was particularly common. This, at times, led to abuse, divorce, legal consequences, and abandonment.

In addition, the number of uninsured was high compared to nationally reported figures. Too few culturally and linguistically competent providers, cultural taboos against services, and lack of knowledge about mental health treatment options were also major barriers. Limited English speakers encountered some of the greatest barriers. Mexico was the most common source of mental health and physical self-healthcare. This option provided some needed access. But there are fewer safeguards around some treatments and medications in Mexico as compared to the US. This, for example, sparked concerns (e.g., among physicians) about the use of medications that can be obtained in Mexico but that are not approved in the US.

Project *Salud Libre* demonstrated that it is important to look at specific communities within a larger country as we assess immigrant needs. While both environments are in the US, rural communities tend to have little in common with large metropolitan areas. Both deserve nuanced attention to their unique conditions. For example, the interaction among cultures when immigrants come to New York City versus California's Imperial Valley is likely to be quite different. This prompts the need for different types of community development.

The methods we used for Project *Salud Libre* and Project *Salaam* had some things in common. While addressing different locations and immigrant groups, both included professionals from various backgrounds and with a variety of expertise (e.g., academia, clinical practice, and community healthcare) to address local Southern California problems. This combination showed how team members from various backgrounds can tackle problems if they work together as equals.

A different kind of project:

While the two examples described above entailed community-based needs assessment, we also conducted others that focused on systems used to qualify healthcare providers. Our basic question was: do such qualifying systems assess if providers are well trained in cultural circumstances that impact care?

Cultural Competence in the Licensure of Health Care Professionals[103] was a project sponsored by the US Department of Health & Human Services, Office of Minority Health (OMH). Our work investigated the degree to which cultural competence was assessed by the licensure processes and examinations of various health service disciplines.

"Cultural Competence" entailed the degree to which major national healthcare licensure examinations and other procedures include a) content valid questions that address human diversity, and b) initial and on-going validity checks designed to assess whether examination procedures and/or artifacts had any adverse impact on members of linguistically and culturally distinct groups. In addition, the report included a review of existing approaches to oral and practical examinations, and an assessment of perceptions about examination content, fairness, and other relevant issues among candidates from culturally and linguistically distinct groups. Finally, the project made research and policy recommendations and identified existing barriers that impede efforts to improve cultural competence in licensure.

Given OMH's mission to improve and protect the health of racial and ethnic minority populations, the report largely focused on such groups. Our project did not cover examinations for disciplines such as chiropractic, optometry, pharmacy, physical therapy, respiratory care, and vocational nursing. Rather, it focused on seven major professional fields in order to begin a process that highlights the range of testing approaches and practices currently in use. These were tests for medical doctors, osteopathic doctors, psychologists, registered nurses, dentists, social workers, and nationally certified counselors. It was our hope that the report would stimulate broader research and discussion on cultural competence in the licensing of health care professionals.

The following background considerations prompted our involvement in the project at the time: While providing culturally competent healthcare is every provider's obligation, available literature points out that a diverse healthcare workforce is likely to enhance and broaden service access. We, for example, know that Latino and Black health care providers tend to work with greater numbers of patients from traditionally underserved groups than do their White counterparts. Studies have also pointed out that, other factors being equal, an ethnic match between provider and patient/client tends to increase consumer satisfaction and service utilization.[104] Some educational programs and institutions have thus increased their emphasis on "pipeline" efforts that attract diverse talent to health care careers (e.g., Hispanic Centers of Excellence). Conversely, existing literature asserts that policies hindering the recruitment and education of health care workers from culturally distinct populations reduce access to health care for those at the lower end of the socioeconomic spectrum and among so-called "minorities."[105] The ongoing shortage of healthcare professionals from linguistically and culturally distinct groups makes these issues particularly critical.[106] (For a broader discussion on the topic, please see Chapter 10.)

One area of healthcare that has been substantially under-investigated is the role that professional licensing methods and procedures play in promoting or hindering efforts to increase a culturally competent provider base. Existing research indicates that people from various ethnic groups fare differently on licensing examinations. For example, Dawson-Saunders, Iwamoto, Ross, and colleagues[107] report that the United States Medical Licensing Examination (abbreviated USMLE), Step 1, a portion of the licensing process for medical doctors, exhibits lower pass rates for non-White culturally distinct groups (49% for Black persons, 66% for Latinos, and 88% for Whites). The National Board of Medical Examiners[108] counters that, after multiple attempts, almost all candidates pass eventually (100% Whites, 98% for Latinos and 93% of Black persons). Studies in other disciplines, Werner[109] reported that non-White applicants in California passed the nationally given Examination for Professional Practice in Psychology (EPPP) at well under half the rate of their White counterparts. Similar trends have been found in nursing licensure examinations.[110]

Through this project, we learned that there were major differences in the ways various examinations address human diversity content and process. For example, the National Council of State Boards of Nurses, developer of the primary RN exam, statistically validated test items by gender and major ethnic group. Disparate performance triggered a review that could lead to item removal. English as a second language background was also tracked. Prominent exams for other disciplines (e.g., social work) also checked performance by ethnicity and gender. In contrast, examination developers in psychology, osteopathic medicine, and dentistry reported no such procedures.

In part, we recommended that licensing jurisdictions and licensing exam developers not already doing so collect voluntary ethnic/racial and ESL status data from their candidates. We advised that human diversity / culture-based exam items should be tracked to learn how frequently they are included. Exam developers were encouraged to include the previously described National Standards on Culturally and Linguistically Appropriate Services (CLAS) as content in ethics and other appropriate exam sections. Finally, we recommended that licensing jurisdictions that use oral, clinical, or practical skills tests should train examiners in cultural competence.

This project specifically investigated one element within US healthcare. But the methods we used can also be translated into other areas. Systematic analyses of rules and procedures, as well as how they are applied in real life, can improve success in government, business, and many other areas. As discussed in Chapter 10, the COVID-19 pandemic has demonstrated that nations are best served by working together on worldwide problems. Using an organized approach to learn where barriers to progress exist can help us get rid of obstacles that interfere with such efforts.

The projects discussed above hoped to achieve broad-based changes in systems and methods that serve diverse populations. But what does real-life work in a clinical setting look like? There are times we need to tease out what is culture, what is basic personality, and how they all interact together. The vignette below provides a case example.

> ### What is Cultural and what is "just" psychological? A nuanced example (Dolores Rodríguez-Reimann)
>
> For doctors like Joachim and I who often work with immigrant populations, culture is the lens and filter through which we understand much of our patients' experiences. Yet, there are times where culture is an important factor, but not in the most predominant way. We hope the following story will illustrate this point.
>
> Morgan was an attractive young woman who grew up in the greater Washington District of Columbia (DC) area. When she first came to me, she stated that her main goal of therapy was seeking help for, in her words, "struggles with cultural issues." Morgan believed that her own personal cultural background was Italian and Irish. But there had been "so many generations in between" her and the period that her ancestors immigrated to the United States. Consequently, Morgan described herself as "basically American." Her father, a captain in the Air Force had traveled throughout his career, often taking the family with him. According to Morgan by the time she was 13 years old, she had already lived in 14 countries. Her mother reportedly became pregnant in one country but then delivered Morgan in a different one.
>
> Cultural issues that Morgan reportedly was struggling with had to do with a situation at work. Morgan had made a career in the financial industry and given her international experience, she was fairly comfortable traveling to various countries. According to Morgan, she

was quite successful at her job. She went on to describe that a couple of years back (in late 2017), a longtime friend and mentor, along with two other colleagues, decided that they would pool their talents and start a new company that engaged in international consulting. They asked Morgan if she wanted to be a part of the start-up.

Morgan was very excited and hopeful that once the new company "took off," she and her friends would have new and interesting adventures. Through Morgan's travels, she had made many friends internationally. One friend, in particular, was Isabel, also in the financial industry. Isabel was a middle-aged lady that Morgan had grown very fond of. Isabel was born and raised in Spain and considered herself a cultural mix herself with a Spanish mother while her father had been born and raised in Germany. When Morgan and Isabel met nearly 10 years earlier, Isabel was married and was raising two boys Alejandro and Adrián. By the time Morgan made her first appointment to see me, both of Isabel's sons had grown into adulthood.

Morgan and Isabel had met at a conference and, from the beginning, they felt they had a connection. They became fast friends and often consulted with each other regarding work. As friends, they also supported each other through personal trials and experiences. Isabel was a constant friend, easy to reach out to when Morgan's mother succumbed to cancer just three years ago. After Isabel's divorce in 2017 and her two boys had gone off to college Isabel considered emigrating to the US to start a new chapter in her life. Morgan felt that was a great idea, especially given Isabel's particular expertise and experience. Perhaps she thought Isabel could join Morgan and her colleagues with their new business venture. Morgan shared this idea with her colleagues and friends and soon they all agreed that Isabel had something to contribute to the start-up. With her many international connections and fluency in four languages, Isabel could quickly be an important asset to the consulting firm's goals and objectives. Isabel had been to the United States only once before when she visited New York City for a couple of weeks. But she was not familiar with Southern California. However, Morgan believed that Isabel could make the transition and could adapt. Morgan spoke with Isabel and soon there were plans drawn up to help Isabel integrate herself with Morgan's working group and plan for Isabel's immigration to the United States.

By the time Morgan came to see me for therapy, it had been six months since Isabel immigrated to San Diego, California. The original agreement between Morgan and Isabel was that Isabel would take over the planning and development for the company's European Division. Morgan and her colleagues would help support Isabel through her transition to the US. To that end, and to not deplete Isabel's savings unnecessarily, Isabel would live in a guesthouse at Morgan's home rent-free. Another colleague would lend Isabel a car so that she could drive around and acclimate herself to her new surroundings. According to the plan, Isabel was interested in staying in the US yet wanted to visit Spain once she got settled here. This fit perfectly with the start-up's objectives as well.

English had not been a problem for Isabel since along with Spanish, German, and Russian, English was one of four languages, she had mastered. Yet, according to Morgan soon after Isabel arrived, problems started to surface. Isabel found it difficult to focus on projects that were handed to her and seemed distracted by issues and problems with her adult sons back in Spain. This involved issues that appeared trivial to Morgan, like what kind of clothing her sons preferred, and who they dated. Also, while Isabel's divorce had been finalized months earlier, there seem to be constant and continued interest in the comings and goings of her ex-husband. According to Morgan, Isabel would often come to the office late in the morning upset and crying about "all" of the situations "back home." And while Morgan and the others at the office were sympathetic, soon it became evident Isabel needed closer supervision to help her remain "on track" and focused on her agreed-upon responsibilities at work.

In addition, as part of her integration at work, Isabel began to form relationships with individuals that were in Morgan's greater working network. So often, Isabel would spend time with friends, colleagues, and acquaintances of Morgan. Soon though, Morgan began to hear through the "grapevine" that Isabel had been complaining about activities and tasks she was assigned to do at the start-up. Rumors began to surface that Isabel was not being supported and was treated unfairly. The complaints were subtle enough as to not sound entirely ungrateful. Nevertheless they generated sympathy and questions from people who knew Morgan and her colleagues. When Morgan and her colleagues started to hear this feedback, they initially attributed it to the fact that Isabel was "new here," "far away from home," and "having a difficult time adjusting to her new environment." Soon, however, compassion and sympathy began to transition into questions regarding Isabel's true motivations and outright resentment towards her. Before you knew it, untruths and outright lies, accusations, and blame by Isabel became constant issues discussed in "team meetings" between Morgan and her colleagues. It also became apparent that Isabel would find all kinds of reasons why she did not and could not follow-up and deliver on work expectations made of her.

Needless to say, all of this was very stressful for Morgan because ultimately, she felt responsible for introducing Isabel to the group. Morgan also felt compassion towards Isabel. It seemed to her that Isabel was having "a hard time" acclimating to her new life despite the fact that Isabel had repeatedly stated she had exactly what she wanted; coming to the US and working for a new and interesting company.

How much of this is cultural Morgan would ask me in session, and how much of it is something else? Morgan often said "...sometimes I feel so sorry for Isabel and I just want to help. And then there are other times when I get really angry and say enough already maybe you (Isabel) don't need to work with us if you are that unhappy." Morgan wanted me to help her sort out her own feelings and wanted to figure out the best way to negotiate her friendship with Isabel and protecting the integrity of her workgroup in a way that "was fair to everyone."

After a couple of sessions, Morgan began to feel "less stressed" in her dealings with Isabel. Morgan became more certain about her own feelings, and we practiced how Morgan could set clearer boundaries whenever she was faced with Isabel's projection of her own personal issues. Morgan was also encouraged that Isabel had met someone, a male friend. Isabel had developed her own new social connections and seemed optimistic and more hopeful about her future. Yet having a "new boyfriend" further distracted Isabel from her work. She would often leave the office unannounced and at times would not show up to work at all.

Then after about five weeks of meeting with Morgan regularly, something happened that completely changed our work. Our goals for therapy shifted. According to Morgan, it all took place over a long holiday weekend. Isabel and her new man, Albert, decided to move in together. This was a move that Morgan did not honestly object to, even though she felt it was "too early" for Isabel to consider that option. So, at about 3:00 AM on a Holiday Monday, Morgan received a call from Isabel asking Morgan to bail her out of jail since she had been arrested the night before on an assault charge in a domestic violence situation. Apparently, Isabel and Albert had been drinking alcohol and an argument/fight broke out. According to the story Isabel grabbed a knife and threatened to stab herself as well as Albert. While fortunately, no one was severely injured, Isabel did manage to throw a glass at Albert, hitting him on the side of his face. When neighbors heard the commotion, they called the police, and eventually, it was Isabel who had been arrested.

Needless to say, Morgan was in shock, devastated, and really angry that she got "dragged into" such a difficult and messy situation. Morgan was clear that "she was finally done with Isabel" and "that was the last straw." For Morgan, it was now a matter of how to end the relationship with Isabel in the most amicable way while minimizing risk to herself, her colleagues, and the company. While it is unethical from my professional perspective to diagnose a person who I do not personally evaluate, it was clear to me that, if I was to help Morgan through this situation, part of my work was to help her navigate and understand how to work through cultural contexts but also differentiate between them and what clearly appeared to be prompted by Isabel's personality traits.

I asked Morgan if, over the course of their friendship, she had ever witnessed Isabel engage in dangerous or impulsive behavior that Morgan felt was somehow "out of bounds." Morgan reported that she felt Isabel had a long history of difficult relationships where friends and relatives would be in and out of Isabel's life, often due to the most minor problems or perceived slights. Morgan also said that, at times, Isabel was "a little overly dramatic" in her emotional response to certain setbacks. But for Morgan, that was "...just how Isabel was..." and in Morgan's words "...I don't judge people for who they are..."

While it is true that different cultures allow for differences in the range of emotional expression, (on a personal note, I often describe myself as a highly "passionate Latina"), there are personality traits and styles of coping that can become difficult no matter where you come from. A personality style that is problematic has the potential to become a disorder marked by difficult and complicated interpersonal relationships, and issues with a low self-image. In some cases, such styles of coping can become a serious mental illness marked by unstable moods and impulsive behavior. In mental health, there are a series of dysfunctional styles of coping that once they become rigid, they can lead to full-blown personality disorders that negatively impact a person's overall mental health and wellbeing.

According to what Morgan was describing, Isabel had a coping style in which individuals like her regularly have problems with relationships, family, work-life, long-term planning, and self-identity. In extreme cases, people who exhibit dysfunctional coping attempts can experience intense bouts of anger, depression, and anxiety. In extreme cases, this can lead to self-injury or suicide, as well as drug and or alcohol abuse. Since I never met or treated Isabel, I had no direct evidence regarding her behavior so I could not diagnose her with a personality disorder or anything else. I did, however, have enough information to help Morgan sort out what was cultural and what appeared to clearly be Isabel's personality issues.

In the end, Isabel moved in with Albert and decided that working with Morgan and her colleagues was not a "good fit" for her. Both Morgan and Isabel decided to remain friends. Yet there was no expectation that the relationship between Morgan and Isabel would continue as it once had.

In analyzing this case example, I would like to point out a few observations: While culture is a major lens through which I conceptualize people's experience, I felt very early on that there was a lot more than "cultural issues" going on for Morgan and her friend Isabel. While people who immigrate often experience transition issues, the types of problems Isabel was having were not consistent with the general immigrant experience. For example, immigrants, as a whole, are usually willing to work hard and do not look for excuses to "pull their weight." Immigrants who come from cultures where family identity is important usually express attitudes that foster a continuation of those family ties. Yet in the case of Isabel, it appeared that the opposite was taking place. Isabel seemed to be creating problems by inserting herself inappropriately into the lives of her two adult sons and with her ex-husband. A final factor in my assessment of the circumstances, in this case, was that I felt that Morgan was strongly invested in Isabel's success. As such, Morgan was willing to look at herself (including seeking the help of a clinical psychologist) to make sure she was doing everything possible from her end to help her friend. Yet for Isabel, there seemed to be little consideration or appreciation of the efforts made by Morgan to help her.

Given wars and torture that some other immigrant groups have escaped from, Isabel's and Morgan's problems may seem trivial. But their problems were important to the people in this story. As we have said throughout this book, immigrants come from all circumstances and backgrounds. In addition to describing an example in which what was cultural and what were personality dysfunction, this story points out that all people in various forms of distress deserve our respect and, to the degree possible, our assistance.

Questions to Consider

When you consider your own experience, are there any instances where you feel that you were treated in a way that was respectful of who you are and how you see yourself? Was there a situation when that was not the case? How did you deal with it? If you could go back and do it again, what would you do differently?

Recommendations

- Seek mentorships with people who have had similar experiences, have overcome hardships, and have thus "walked the walk."
- Participate in research/clinical trials. This may inform you about the specific health needs of your own community. It may also allow you to contribute to solutions that address those needs.
- Develop contacts for future education/employment/advocacy.
- Volunteer in organizations geared toward immigrant services.
- If you are a student, seek internships that work with culturally distinct populations. Many colleges and universities have also adopted an approach called service learning through civic engagement. This takes student and instructors out of the classroom and tasks them to develop and carry out a wide variety of community projects. Such a project can certainly provide opportunities to work with immigrants from various backgrounds.

- If you are a small or start-up business, consider alliance with other small businesses made up of people from different cultures. Often such joint ventures allow enterprises to get contracts and customers that one business alone could not reach. When several start-up enterprises share a joint space or are otherwise in close proximity, this is often called a small business incubator.

Resources

- The full National Standards for Culturally and Linguistically Appropriate Services (CLAS) in Health and Health Care can be found online at: https://thinkculturalhealth.hhs.gov/clas.
- A UK-based cultural competence toolkit can be found at: https://www.diversecymru.org.uk/wp-content/uploads/Cultural-Competency-Toolkit.pdf.

9

GROUP FOR IMMIGRANT RESETTLEMENT & ASSESSMENT (GIRA)

As described in earlier chapters, our work as psychologists often entails forensic evaluations for immigration cases (e.g., extreme hardship cases; asylum applications; spousal abuse cases, etc.). In a different but related field, we have conducted university-based public health and psychological research. Both research and clinical services have largely focused on culturally and linguistically distinct populations (particularly Latino, East African, and Middle Eastern immigrants and refugees). This work is ongoing. Such efforts are rewarding in that they can positively impact a variety of people.

In short, we are always ready for a new project. Each is an adventure. For us, the present questions are: How do we use our experience in some additional constructive way? Can we help create systematic approaches that aid immigrants in their efforts to acclimate to a new country? If so, how do we do that? Is there a methodical approach that people who work with immigrants will find useful?

These questions prompted us to form the Group for Immigrant Resettlement & Assessment (GIRA) several years ago. GIRA is a multidisciplinary entity made up of clinical and social psychologists, researchers, career development specialists, leaders of community-based organizations, and others who have relevant expertise. Our group's mission is to create, and then use, psychometric measures that add relevant information to immigration processes that allow for informed choices when helping immigrants. In this context, our interest is in professional, nuanced, and non-political approaches that contribute to solutions in these types of circumstances.

As clinicians or social service providers, we generally listen to our clients' needs and circumstances to come up with an individualized assistance (or treatment) plan. GIRA's effort is essentially the same. It includes development of an instrument, the Successful Immigrant Resettlement Inventory (SIRI), which assesses primary dimensions discussed in this book and uses that information to identify an individual's unique needs and circumstances.

Specifically, SIRI includes basic demographic information and then addresses acculturative/psychosocial stressors, openness to acculturative and adaptive processes, psychological and behavioral tendencies (including personality traits and resilience), physical health status, and employment/career orientations. Both immigrants and people who help them can then use this information to develop a comprehensive and personalized roadway to success.

We further believe that this type of measurement can have uses that assist legal procedures used in immigration cases. For example, asylum seekers often lack documents that "prove" their difficult history. Verifying psychological symptoms that are consistent with trauma-related disturbances can add credibility to legitimate asylum seekers.

In short, SIRI can act as an assessment and service planning tool used by a non-governmental organization (NGOs) community-based organizations (CBOs), government entities, educational systems, and others. With results in hand, people who work on the front lines can help immigrants by identifying and using the right services. This approach can enhance and enable a smoother acculturative process by assisting people to overcome acculturative and resettlement barriers. For example, a SIRI report has the potential to enhance the quality of life and positive social contributions by developing effective employability/educational plans for immigrants who need this type of help.

On a broader level, information from SIRI can inform policy. It can pinpoint what types of services are most needed in specific areas and for specific people. That can then help us put money and other resources where they will do the most good.

At the same time, assessing immigrants in multiple ways can also raise difficult questions. What if there are people with criminal and even terrorist risk factors in the group? SIRI is not a measure that can spot a terrorist in a crowd. But, if applied properly, it may point to ways in which radicalization risks, particularly among people who feel they have no future, can be lowered.

Many people, especially from Middle Eastern, North African, and other predominantly Muslim countries hesitate to talk about radicalization, and for good reasons. They are worried about being stereotyped because that has happened to them. Many have been victims of terrorists themselves. So they know the dangers involved firsthand. Yet, in their adopted country they are often grouped in with the very people they have fled from. That has to be perplexing at best. Similarly, there are far too many public comments about people from Mexico and

Central America that label the actual victims of criminals as "the" criminals.

Never-the-less, there can also be some real concerns. While a very small number of immigrants are criminals and/or terrorists, we only need to consider the history of attacks in the US, the UK, Spain, France, Austria, and many other countries to know that a few radicals can cause a lot of death and destruction. Given this reality, we need to better understand what the facts around radicalization are. Is there a substantial relationship between criminal acts and immigration? Who is most tempted to join criminal/terrorist groups? Are there things we can do to divert people from such decisions?

Criminal Activity Among Immigrants

Arguably, the amount of criminal activity among foreign-born persons is less than that among the native-born population in several countries. Information from the US Bureau of Justice Statistics shows that non-citizen inmates in state and federal prisons comprise less than 6% of the total prison population. Alex Nowrasteh, director of immigration studies at the Cato Institute has concluded that "the criminal conviction and arrest rates for immigrants (even in case of the undocumented) were well below those of native-born Americans."[111] An overall analysis of 51 US studies published on the subject from 1994–2014 found that, if anything, immigration tends to be associated with reduced rather than increased crime rates.[112] The reasons for this trend remain poorly understood. But there is substantial evidence that it has been consistently true in recent history.[113]

Research on this topic in other countries across the world has shown mixed results. No relationship between immigration status and crime has, for example, been found in Australia.[114]

In Italy, studies found that foreign-born persons tended to commit slightly more robberies from 1990–2003.[115] But the overall crime rate among non-native residents then dropped by 65% between 2007 and 2016.[116] Similarly in the UK, one study noted that the local prison population was not increasing substantially due to any incidents of a serious crime committed by foreign persons.[117]

On the other hand, research in Germany, Norway, Spain, and a few other countries have reported higher crime rates attributed to immigrants, though in some instances these increases were relatively small.[118,119,120]

Is there a way to fix things if crime rates are a problem? Some studies in the EU have found that granting legal status to undocumented persons can reduce crime.[121] This may happen because legal status opens up more economic opportunities and generally reduces fears and frustrations for people.

Crimes Against Immigrants

On the other side of this picture is the concern that immigrants are too often the victims rather than the perpetrators of crime. People fleeing from war and persecution can be quite vulnerable to abuse and exploitation. For example 75% or more Syrian refugees are at-risk women and children. Even if they make it to refugee camps, many fear they will be abused by staff and others there. Some female refugees end up being sexually exploited under the premise that this is the only way they can survive financially.[122]

Closely related to this situation is sex trafficking. The American Civil Liberties Union (ACLU) reports that in the US, almost all victims of sex trafficking are immigrant women with an average age of 20 years. Women with less education, limited

English speaking ability, and no knowledge of US legal employment protections are particularly at risk.[123]

Other parts of the world also report the victimization of immigrants. One study in South Africa, for example, found that 85% of the foreign-born people they assessed had been victims of crimes. The most common crimes were break-ins of homes and lootings of immigrant businesses.[124]

Additional types of criminal activity encountered by immigrants include being robbed while migrating and experiencing hate crimes. Yet our research as well as other studies shows that victims rarely report such incidents to authorities for fear of drawing attention to themselves and being victimized even more.

Radicalization and Terrorism

Terrorism is constantly in the news. While the number of people involved is relatively small, we all know that one person who commits a violent act can create havoc for many others. Yet, as previously noted, is also true that based on their religion and dress, some immigrant groups are too often stereotyped across the board as "terrorists."[65]

The actual relationship between immigration and terrorism has not been sufficiently researched. A 2016 study did find that higher levels of migration were associated with a lower level of terrorism in the host country. At the same time, migrants who are specifically from terror-prone states do increase the risk of terrorism in the host country.[125] Some of these latter findings may not even involve foreign-born persons. When we were at a 2019 conference in London we, for example, heard anecdotal concerns that ISIS fighters, who had been driven from their territory in Syria, were coming to the UK. But these were not necessarily "foreigners." Some were UK passport holders who were returning "home."

The topic of radicalization is highly complex. First, it is important to note that the expression of "radical" or "extremist" beliefs does not automatically mean the person or persons involved are going to commit violence. In fact, among some nations including the US, the expression of radical ideas, without the threat of or advocacy for violence, is protected in the Constitution. Secondly, violent terrorist acts have been committed in the name of multiple causes. These include homegrown as well as international roots. The August 3, 2019, mass shooting in our old hometown of El Paso, Texas was not perpetrated by immigrants but was prompted by anti-Mexican hate. In addition, the US Federal Bureau of Investigation (FBI) called growing domestic violent extremism the number one terrorist threat in 2021.[126]

To counter violent radicalism, we need to understand terrorists' motivations, attitudes, world views, and thought processes. "Understanding" doesn't excuse or find rationales for their behaviors. Rather, the well-worn Sun Tzu quote: (paraphrasing) "know yourself, know your enemy, and you shall win a hundred battles" without loss points to the wisdom of identifying what we are facing to find effective counters. Behavioral scientists (e.g., psychologists) have much to contribute but have been underutilized in this effort.[127]

What are some basics in understanding radicalization? First, it is important to know that radical extremists do not all fit one profile. Those in recruitment and leadership positions are, for example, unlikely to go on suicide missions themselves though they try to attract others who are willing to do so.[128] Secondly, terrorism is not necessarily connected with mental disorders though that tends to be a common presumption.[129,130]

But there are some known risk factors. Those who are susceptible to recruitment by terrorist groups often lack self-confidence and feel themselves to be rejected by greater society. They believe that they have no path to a good future. Then along comes a recruiter who promises them belonging, a type of family and brotherhood, and a central role in the creation of a great and just new world. Even if they die they are promised 1) rewards in the afterlife and 2) that they will be remembered as a martyr. Finally, some radical groups promise to take care of the family members after a "martyr's" death.[128] This "sales pitch" can be profoundly attractive to someone who feels he or she belongs nowhere and has no future.

What can be done to counter this kind of radicalization risk? One of the most interesting views we have heard is from the Soufan Center. Rather than a social service organization, this group is largely made up of law enforcement and intelligence professionals who have worked in national and international agencies.

The Soufan Center's 2017 publication "Syria; The Humanitarian Security Nexus"[47] argues that, for refugees, humanitarian and security concerns cannot be addressed separately. Rather, they are two faces of the same coin. People who have hope for acceptance, opportunities, and a positive future are much more able to resist the false promises made by radical groups. This can not only help immigrants themselves but can have positive ripple effects for their children and children's children. Social and behavioral scientists have echoed similar themes by emphasizing that positive social and community connections, support, and cooperation can help thwart violent extremism.[131]

Providing multi-faceted, organized, integrated, and coordinated avenues for immigrants can offer them a ladder to earned success. Support and guidance is a constructive rather than punitive action. But it requires that we have a good up-front assessment of peoples' needs and circumstances. GIRA seeks to foster such an assessment.

Questions to Consider

- If you were the victim of a crime would you feel comfortable notifying the police or other authorities? If not, what law enforcement actions would give you more confidence that reporting a crime would have a good outcome for you?
- Do you feel that you have been subjected to prejudice and hate?
- What allows you to persevere, even if you have had negative experiences?

Resources

Many organizations help members of radical groups that have become disillusioned and want to leave that life. These organizations treat both international terrorists and local right-wing hate groups.

To find out more about countering violent extremism, please see a review of the topic at: https://www.mei.edu/publications/deradicalization-programs-and-counterterrorism-perspective-challenges-and-benefits.

10

THE COVID-19 PANDEMIC

A s we write this book in our California home, we have been locked down twice so far. Our governor reports that, given present COVID-19 infection, disease, and mortality rates, it is in our best public health interest to continue restricting our activities. The US has had lockdowns, over-crowded hospitals and more deaths per capita than most anywhere else in the world. COVID-19 is mutating (often described as "variants"), and when this pandemic will fully subside is yet unclear.

Since both of us were researchers at San Diego State University's Graduate School of Public Health for a combined 22 years (1997–2008) we take pandemic data and the guidance of infectious disease experts and scientists very seriously. We have only ventured out when we have had to. In his chapter we will further highlight some points outlined in earlier parts of this book and speak to how these issues have played themselves out so far using COVID-19 as an example.

The Coronavirus (SARS-CoV-2) that has caused the COVID-19 pandemic of 2019, 2020, 2021, and possibly beyond, has had a profound impact on our world. It is an unprecedented event in our lifetime. Yet, we know historically that pandemics are not new to the human experience. About 5 million people died of what was probably smallpox in the Roman Empire between 165 and 168 AD. Marcus Aurelius, Emperor at the time, called it the "Plague of Galen." The disease is thought to have been brought to Rome by troops who fought in Western Asia. In other words, like infectious diseases today, it spread across broad regions through human contact. The Bubonic Plague killed an estimated 25 million people between 1347 and 1352. More recently, influenza outbreaks such as the Spanish Flu have caused around 50 million deaths up to 1919.

There have certainly been other pandemics between the early 1900s and COVID-19. These have included the SARS, the Swine Flu, Ebola, MERS, and AIDS. But, in an age where we tend to assume that modern medicine will guard our health, none has had a universal impact matching COVID-19. Aside from the direct physical consequence of the disease, we have experienced a myriad of economic and social disruptions in our daily lives. Not surprisingly this has caused much distress.

Researchers using US-wide data, for example, found that in April and May of 2020, adults were three times more likely to report anxiety, depression, or both than they had over the first half of 2019.[132] In addition, a 2020 Rand Corporation study found a recent 54% increase in US national alcohol sales, compared to pre-COVID figures.[133] Similar patterns have been reported worldwide. At the same time a 2020 World Health Organization (WHO) report concluded that the pandemic has substantially disrupted mental health services, particularly in countries that lack the infrastructure to fully use telemedicine as an alternative to in-person help.[134]

A pandemic is defined as a disease that has spread across several countries and, in that process, has affected a large number of people. Since it knows no international borders, migration patterns and outcomes are important considerations. This includes health and mental health vulnerabilities faced by immigrants.

At the same time, positive contributions immigrants make to our society during a health crisis cannot be overlooked.

In this chapter we discuss both the contributions immigrants have made to their new societies as well as the risks they face in doing so, during a period when humans are experiencing a worldwide healthcare worker shortage. We will provide recommendations for strategic solutions for the outcomes of pandemics on an international level in the future. This is followed by some real-world examples that show the interplay of COVID-19 and cultural/acculturative factors in clinical practice. Finally we present some questions that you, the reader, can ask yourself.

Immigrant Populations: Impact and Vulnerabilities

Those who track statistics for various populations, tell us that migrant workers tend to be on the frontline on the COVID-19 pandemic response. According to the March 2020 fact sheet from the Migration Policy Institute (MPI), a non-partisan think tank established in 2001, 6 million immigrant workers are helping to keep US residents healthy and fed during this time.[135]

Specifically, MPI reports that immigrants make substantial contributions, both to the healthcare directly and to other essential services. A few specific numbers are as follows: People identified as foreign-born account for a notable percentage of occupations that directly respond to the pandemic. This includes 29% of all physicians and 38% of home health aides. Immigrants also represent a significant number of workers who clean hospital rooms, staff grocery stores and produce food.

In April 2020 MPI also wrote that 2.1 million immigrants in the US work in food production jobs. These jobs include growing, harvesting, processing, and selling food. Foreign-born individuals have an essential role in feeding America. Between 2014 and 2018 they made up 22% of workers in the US food supply chain which involves growing, harvesting, processing, transporting, and selling food to US families.[136]

From field to table, immigrants make up 30% of all agricultural workers, 27% of workers in food production, 17% of transportation workers, 23% of grocery/farm products wholesalers, 37% of the meat processing industry, 34% of workers in commercial bakeries, 31% of fruit and vegetable preserving industry workers, and 26% of workers in seafood processing industries. In the US, an estimated 483,000 foreign-born people also work in grocery stores. This represents 16% of the nearly 3 million grocery retail workers. The current pandemic thus teaches us that many people we consider to have lower skills are actually crucial to the health of an economy and are the key workers that help keep it going through a crisis.[136]

For obvious reasons, the availability of healthcare workers is also an essential consideration during the COVID-19 pandemic. Given that the virus has an international impact, we need to address what this availability looks like on a broad scale.

One source of information is the Organization for Economic Co-operation and Development (OECD), an intergovernmental economic body. The OECD notes that one in six doctors among their 37 member countries has studied abroad. This trend is growing. Over the last decade, the number of foreign-born doctors and nurses increased by 20%. Using specific examples, it is notable that immigrants make up 12% of the United Kingdom's Health Force and comprises 17% of such professionals in the United States. A December 2, 2019 paper by Abbas Adjani concluded that the United Kingdom (UK) has one of the highest numbers of foreign-born doctors and nurses. Among other EU countries, foreign-born doctors accounted for more than 20% of all physicians in Sweden, Denmark, and Germany. Foreign-born nurses account for more than 15% of the overall nursing workforce in Austria, Latvia, and Germany.[137]

Such immigrant professionals are disproportionately employed in pandemic response frontline occupations. In short, migrants are more likely to be on the frontlines of the COVID–19 response than any other health workers.[138]

In summary, a significant number of foreign-born people are employed in food production/service and healthcare jobs. They make a major contribution to our well-being. Yet given the nature of their jobs, these workers are at particular risk of contracting COVID-19. Too often they sacrifice their health and even their lives in the service to others. For example, according to Amnesty International 30.5% of Coronavirus deaths among the 1,077 healthcare workers who had died at that point (September 2020) were born outside the United States.[139]

The Pre-Existing Problem

Even before COVID-19 emerged, statistics showed that there are not enough available healthcare workers. The World Health Organization (WHO), for example, estimates that the global shortage of such workers entails 4.3 million physicians, nurses, and other health professionals. This shortage is often most evident in developing countries since they have a limited number of educational institutions that can train and educate needed professionals. Rural areas can be particularly hard-hit, given their remote locations.

The developed world is also not immune to such problems. There have, for example, been an estimated 44,000 nursing vacancies in the UK. If current trends continue this figure may well reach one hundred thousand (100,000) over the next decade. The 2017 Global Burden of Disease Study further estimated that the United States would need 1 million more nurses by 2021. In terms of US physicians, the projected shortfall has been estimated as somewhere between 46,900 and 121,900 by 2032.[140] In part, this is due to the increasing medical needs of an aging population.

Physicians and nursing shortages have substantially hampered the quality of care. They can shorten the time a provider has to interact with patients, overwork and thus stress available practitioners, increase service wait times, decrease the number of available hospital beds, and drive up healthcare costs.[141] Not surprisingly, the outcome is clinically worse and less timely services for patients.

During the COVID-19 pandemic, healthcare worker shortages are likely to become even more pressing. The need for services is dramatically increased and health workers themselves are becoming infected. Recent figures have, for example, shown that physicians and nurses account for 15% of infections in Wuhan, China, 14% in Spain, and 10% in Italy. According to a September 3, 2020 article by Amnesty International, at least 7,000 health workers had died worldwide after contracting COVID-19 at that point. Among these 1,320 were from Mexico, 1,077 were in the US, 634 were in Brazil, 240 were in South Africa, and 573 were in India.[139] These are the best numbers available as we are writing this book. They will surely continue to increase until the pandemic subsides.

As demonstrated by such numbers, immigrant healthcare workers have essential functions in providing critical care alongside their native-born colleagues, especially during a pandemic. Foreign-born doctors play a particularly large role in providing health care to rural and disadvantaged communities. They also tend to serve more of the elderly and disabled in nursing homes and other long-term care facilities. In the US in 2020 healthcare providers include an estimated 29,000 persons who fell under the Deferred Action for Childhood Arrivals (DACA) policy. How the US immigration policy will impact these workers is unclear. But it is certain that, at present, they play an increasingly critical role in the US healthcare infrastructure.[140]

Given all of the circumstances described above, COVID-19 should be a wake-up call. History teaches us that it is not the last pandemic humanity will encounter. Even in the current pandemic it is likely that additional outbreaks in various parts of the world will occur. Can we learn how to be more prepared? What lessons can we apply? What part do immigrants play in the development of these plans?

Things to Consider

All evidence suggests that pandemics will become increasingly common in the future. This is likely due to increasing global travel and integration, urbanization, changes in land use, and greater use of the natural environment. Given our aging population, more people have underlying medical conditions so they will be more vulnerable to severe and even life-threatening symptoms.

Without intervention, aging and growing populations will meet even larger health worker shortages than they are today. Specifically, the World Health Organization has estimated that by 2030 the world will need an additional 15 million of such workers. Immigrants can help meet these shortfalls.

Are there solutions? As the philosopher, Plato is presumed to have said in ancient Greece, "necessity is the mother of invention." COVID-19 has shown us that traditional barriers limiting foreign-born healthcare workers from practicing their profession in a new country can be overcome. Prompted by the COVID-19 emergency, many jurisdictions have softened the restrictions on foreign-trained and foreign-born health workers in high-income countries to better cope with this crisis. There are reports that health care workers have even been flown to hard-hit countries from overseas (e.g., Chinese, Cuban, and Albanian doctors were sent to Italy). Refugee doctors without local licenses have been called up in Germany and have had their immigration fast-tracked in the United Kingdom. In the United States, New York City allowed foreign-trained doctors to work. There is certainly long-term precedence for accepting international healthcare workers when faced with local shortages. For example, a sizable number of Filipino nurses have migrated to the US, largely stating in the 1960s under what was then called the Exchange Visitor Program.

Here are some basic recommendations for the future:

Recommendations

If we consider facts rather than politics, we have to acknowledge that the COVID-19 pandemic caught the world flat-footed. We were not prepared to prevent, minimize, or effectively treat the disease. To avoid future illness and even death on such a large scale, we must put well-developed and effective systems in place. At a minimum these should 1) include early warning methods that alert us to outbreaks as soon as they occur, 2) track the local and international paths of disease, 3) mobilize ways to limit the spread, 4) keep the public fully informed of known specifics around the disease and how people can protect themselves, 5) have a system that channels treatments and healthcare resources (both providers and materials) to where they are needed most, and 6) activate research that identifies the pathogen including modes of transmission to develop effective preventive measures (e.g. vaccines) and treatments in a timely but safe way.

Some if not all of this requires worldwide coordination. The international experiences immigrants bring to the table can help us make good choices. They can also facilitate good treatment outcomes.

In addition to reducing a basic shortage of providers, foreign-trained physicians, nurses, and other healthcare specialists, and scientists may, for example, have helpful knowledge about the national and cultural circumstances around health in their country of origin. This may include information about the trust or mistrust of vaccines. Persons from different nations have not necessarily experienced conditions like those leading to mistrust of healthcare research among communities of color in the US. Knowledge about different experiences with vaccines across various countries is needed to shape focused outreach efforts.

All of this will require us to re-think our existing laws and policies. In the US, for example, recent policy changes around visas (e.g., the H-1B), have made it harder for medical professionals and scientific experts to enter the country.[142] Rather than imposing barriers, policymakers will need to build systems that smooth the quick movement of health workers. This would allow countries in remission to send health workers where they are most needed at any given time.

Even within some countries, various jurisdictions have varying healthcare licensing requirements and procedures. In the US, for example, providers tend to be licensed by individual states rather than nationally. We highly suspect that this system is driven by regional politics rather than some true quality control. As previously noted, some of these problems were temporarily suspended during the COVID-19 emergency. Presuming that there were no negative consequences, more standardized (and reasonable) requirements should be considered.

One interesting concept is to increase the worldwide availability of healthcare professionals through bilateral training agreements between nations. This would allow universities to train providers in the specific needs and circumstances of more than one country. One such model is the Global Skills Partnership.[142] It allows for the distributions of a labor force to where it is most needed. Countries join to provide integrated technology and financing. In December 2018, 163 states adopted the Global Compact for Migration. Global Skill Partnerships are the only specific policy idea included in this agreement. Overall the partnership entails 6 primary dimensions. These are:

1. It addresses future migration pressures (e.g., integration of foreign professionals into host countries and the fiscal impact involved). Plans can then identify ways to lessen any resulting drain of skilled personnel in the countries of origin.

2. It involves employers in host and home countries who identify and train for specific skills. This improves the overall learning curve of the healthcare workers and thus quickens their access to populations who are most in need.

3. It can form public-private partnerships to effectively train people for semi-skilled occupations that don't require university degrees.

4. It can create or improve worker skill sets before people migrate.

5. It can integrate training for migrants with training for non-migrants in the home country. While that process addresses differing needs, it can also foster broader learning among both groups.

6. It can improve flexibility so that, ideally, skills are adapted to specific home and host-country needs.

Developing a coordinated response to an emergency is not new. In California, various fire departments, for example, support each other as large wildfires emerge. Pandemics require the same approach, just on a larger scale.

Clinical Practice During COVID-19

As we said at the outset of this chapter, COVID-19 has impacted both our physical and mental health. Let us share a couple of real-life examples showing what clinical work with immigrant populations has looked like during the pandemic. Not surprisingly, we have had to adapt our practices while maintaining quality, continuity, and cultural competence as we work with people during this critical time. The following examples are adapted from Dolores Rodríguez-Reimann's work.

At any given point in time, roughly 45 to 70 percent of my clinical practice is made up of immigrant patients. Often, quite a few live and work on both sides of the US-Mexico Border. Many were born in Tijuana, Mexico, and have lived on the Mexican and/or the American side of the border all of their lives. Others are native-born US citizens who, in retirement, live in Mexico due to cheaper housing and the general cost of living there.

This is not surprising since San Diego and Tijuana have a bustling and intertwined economy. The main port of entry connecting both countries is the fourth-busiest land border crossing in the world. Under usual circumstances, roughly 70,000 northbound vehicles and 20,000 northbound pedestrians cross the border each day.

Operating a practice in this environment brings both challenges and rewards. Earlier in this book, you read how cultural traditions including health practices often offer protective factors to immigrant communities, (i.e. eating "*nopales*" a common food in Latino culture). Yet, sometimes cultural traditions can clash with new realities. This can leave individuals and their families in turmoil and distress. The following examples illustrate this point.

Traditions
by Dolores Rodríguez-Reimann

On April 22, 2020, the news was particularly grim. Earlier in the day, as part of our new morning ritual, my family and I sought out the latest information on "the virus." While national trends were improving in some places, other areas were seeing a surge in numbers of people becoming infected, sick and dying. All of this occurred against a growing backdrop of protests in which people clamored to "open the state/country."

That morning San Diego County's Health and Human Services had just announced 15 new deaths from the Coronavirus. News headlines read "highest one-day total to date." The County's new case total was 2,434, which included 87 deaths. My family and I were also alarmed to learn that, according to the latest data, Coronavirus cases had continued to increase faster among South Bay residents than in other areas. Cases in the San Ysidro area grew 111% between April 14 and April 20, increasing from 32 cases to 59. By comparison, the number of Coronavirus cases across the entire San Diego County area was doubling every 24 days. The region of Otay Mesa had 132 cases, the greatest number of any single zip code in the County. National City and Chula Vista, where we live/work had the highest percentage of cases relative to their populations.

Later that day, the news headline and my concerns for health and safety made it into my work, specifically my session with Juan in a very real way. Juan had been my patient for a while, and we had worked through a series of issues. He and his family had immigrated from El Salvador years ago and he was very enthusiastic about living in the US. Juan was only eleven years of age when the tragic events of September 11th, 2001 took place in New York City. This made a significant personal impact on him, and he decided to contribute to America's safety. As he often told me, "I knew then I needed to do something to protect America from evil," in this case terrorism. So, when Juan graduated from a High School he quickly enlisted to join the Marines to "do my part." As a Marine after 9/11, Juan saw his share of pain, devastation, and death. Our work together included dealing with Posttraumatic Stress Disorder (PTSD) that had resulted from those experiences. Juan and I also worked through family of origin and relationship issues that made up our therapeutic contract. In short, Juan is a conscientious young man who tries to do the right thing, even when it becomes difficult.

But something was different during our session on April 22nd, 2020. As soon as we greeted each other via videoconferencing (the best way to provide continuity of care for my patients during the lockdown) I knew something was wrong. He looked visibly upset and disheveled. After our initial pleasantries of hellos, I asked what was distressing him so. He explained that he was very troubled, anxious, and feeling hopeless. He added that he had not been able to sleep in a couple of days and had no appetite. With his ability to work from home, he had previously adapted to the Coronavirus demands for social distancing fairly well. Yet that day posed different challenges. He told me that like most people he had been monitoring the news for the latest public health information regarding the spread of the virus. He too was concerned that the area in which we live saw the greatest number of cases of infection, illness, and death.

Juan, a bachelor, lived alone but maintained a very close relationship with his family of origin. His mother, a homemaker all of her life was in her early seventies, was at particular risk of becoming infected because of problems with diabetes, COPD (Chronic Obstructive Pulmonary Disease), and heart issues. His father, now retired from the US Postal Service, still did "odd jobs" as a handyman. Juan's two younger sisters worked for local department stores. Juan's distress was due because earlier that day he argued with his father. Juan's dad understood the severity of the Coronavirus illness. Yet according to Juan, the dad refused to accept that he needed to "change his routine." Juan was particularly distressed that his father had still not given up showing up to complete the "odd jobs" he had promised to some of his "regulars." Perhaps even more distressing for Juan was the fact his father refused to stop his daily trips to the *"panaderia"* (bakery) for his fresh *"pan dulce"* required for *"la hora del Cafecito."* The dad's trip to the local bakery for the sweetbread needed for his coffee break in the afternoon, a longstanding Latino tradition.

"Meter el pan dulce en el café es un hábito Salvadoreño que Muchos disfrutan" Juan said with tears in his eyes. (Translation: Dipping a piece of sweetbread in your cup of coffee is a Salvadoran practice that many people like my dad enjoy.")

"You know, doctor, my dad gets it. He is trying to do what is right to stay safe and healthy," Juan said, "but there are just some things that he feels he must do, and if he can't do those things, then he questions everything with, 'so what's the point?'..."

"And yes, I understand it," Juan continued, "but then what about my mom and my sisters, then I get very upset because my father is just being selfish. Are his cultural traditions so sacred that he places my mother's health at risk?"

At that point reportedly argument ensued. Juan felt that his father was being too *"terco"* (stubborn) and he would not consider any other point of view.

Juan was left with the dilemma often faced by a bicultural experience and generational differences. He wanted to respect (show *"respeto"*) to his father and the value of his traditions. But Juan also felt that the exercise of such traditions was placing the rest of the family at unnecessary risk of falling sick with COVID-19.

Two Countries

Alejandra, her two younger siblings, and their mother had immigrated to San Diego from Tijuana, Mexico in 2000. Alejandra was a nurse by training and an older sister to her youngest sibling Carolina. In 2019, when Carolina was diagnosed with breast cancer, Alejandra became her main caregiver at home. As an oncology nurse at UCSD (University of California San Diego Cancer Center) she was well-qualified to provide that help. After treatments, Carolina beat cancer. But, in the process, she lost her job. As a result, both Carolina and their elderly mother had to relocate from San Diego back to Tijuana, Mexico where the cost of living was significantly cheaper. While family members now lived in different countries, they remained close and often visited each other back and forth as do many families along the US-Mexico border.

Then in the early spring of 2020 COVID-19 disrupted everything. For Alejandra and her family, it was particularly distressing. Alejandra an essential worker, continued to make her hospital rounds at UCSD. Her mother and sister did the best they could while in Tijuana. Border crossings were restricted to essential travel by both the United States and Mexican governments. Alejandra, working long hour shifts at the hospital, did not have the energy and felt it was risky at best to visit her mother and sister for fear of exposing them to the virus. Yet, Carolina and the mother had their own challenges while living in Tijuana. After a slow start, the local Tijuana government followed San Diego's lead in having people work remotely and instituting stay in place and social distancing measures to contain the spread of the virus among the population.

Recently Alejandra's anxiety and panic attacks were driven by concern for her welfare (becoming infected with Coronavirus while working at the hospital), getting sick, and not being able to provide financially for herself and her family living in Mexico. Such concerns were worsened by the frustration that both Carolina and the mother had become convinced that if they stuck with traditional remedies of *"te de manzanilla"* (chamomile tea), *"cucharadas de vinagre"* (drinking apple cider vinegar), *and "sobadas con alcohol"* body rubdowns with alcohol, they would be protected from "the virus." Alejandra and I had shared many conversations where we believe and support the notion that traditional medicine and remedies are helpful, especially if the patient believes in their benefit. But in this case, Alejandra and I agreed that her family's faith in these traditional practices would leave them with a false sense of security and place them at greater risk of becoming exposed, infected, and sick with COVID-19. This was particularly distressing for Alejandra since bouts with cancer had left her sister Carolina with a compromised immune system. Her mother was also at high, risk given her age and health circumstances. As a healthcare provider on the front lines, Alejandra saw the real devastation COVID-19

> could bring. Yet she felt helpless in caring for her family when, in her own words, "they needed me most."

As I consider a post-COVID-19 future of my private practice, constantly updated by guidance from the Center for Disease Control (CDC), the American Psychological Association (APA), and others I think about what our ethical and moral responsibility will entail as we potentially reopen our offices and get back to "normal."

Before the ink dries on this book and all of the specific recommendations/timelines have been worked out, I realize and mourn that my practice will have changed significantly for the foreseeable future. No longer can I afford my *"caluroso abrazo"* a common traditional greeting with my patients, especially those who are older and immune-compromised. My husband, whose practice entails services to many refugee patients, can often have four to six family and extended family members show up with the patient for scheduled appointments. It's an East African norm.

Physical distancing will no doubt interfere with such habits and have a dampening impact on the work we conduct. And while I mourn the loss of what "used to be," I believe that together with my patients we can create ways of connecting and navigate a future where we can retain that which is essential to who we are in a safe new way.

Questions to Consider

- How has the COVID-19 pandemic impacted your life?
- What about the life of your loved ones?

- As an immigrant, how has that identity impacted the way you needed to deal with the difficulties associated with COVID-19?
- What coping strategies have worked or not worked for you?
- What role do you want to play in a post-pandemic society?
- What will help you achieve that goal?
- What can you do? If you are in the healthcare field, can you advocate for change within your profession, its associations, and licensing bodies? Even if you are not in healthcare, how can you advocate for such change with your elected officials?

EPILOGUE

Many well-developed theories, research outcomes, and professional experiences never make it into the public discourse. They remain in journals and occupation-specific books that have lots of technical jargon and are hard to read let alone understand for the average layperson. This is true for the literature on immigration as it is in other areas.

We hope that this book makes professional information about common immigration experiences more accessible. We have also mixed in some examples from our own lives and work to illustrate how abstract concepts can be understood in the real world.

What are the major points we hope people take away from this book? Migrations have happened since there have been people on planet Earth. There are no indications that this will decrease, let alone stop, as global interconnections become an increasing reality. Climate change may also be a growing factor that prompts migrations.

Fortunately, immigration is a good thing. It can revitalize our societies. As US President John F. Kennedy once remarked: "Everywhere immigrants have enriched and strengthened the fabric of American life." In part, statistics cited in this book tell us that, particularly with high-need refugees, we need to make an up-front investment. But they also tell us that, if we do so wisely, the ultimate benefits far outweigh the initial costs.

At the same time, immigration brings many challenges, both for the migrants themselves and their adopted countries. People leave their country of origin for many reasons. Some move because they want to work with colleagues who share their scientific or professional interests. Some come for greater financial opportunities in an increasingly global economy. And some come to escape crime, poverty, war, and persecution.

Despite such diversity of people and reasons for migrating, immigrants share some universal challenges. Moving anywhere new can be stressful under the best of circumstances. People are often required to learn new languages, customs, practices, diets, and even what side of the road they're supposed to drive on. Certain skills are just needed to function in a new world. But there is good news. Acculturation research has shown that learning new skills does not automatically require us to give up our core personal identity.

For both the immigrants' and broader society's sake, we need to learn how we can best have an individualized but coordinated system that helps new arrivals integrate into broader society. This includes smoothing occupational transitions, eliminating mental and physical healthcare barriers, fostering immigrants' resilience, and overcoming personal biases toward people who look different to us and what we're used to. This does not mean we have to be naïve and just let everyone into our doors. There are bad actors in the world, and we must remain vigilant to that reality. But we can also take steps to reduce the likelihood that people who feel they have no future are sucked into the "false advertising" put out by criminal and radical groups.

These types of efforts are in all of our own best interests. As most recently demonstrated by the COVID-19 pandemic, we have shortages in all kinds of critical occupations including health care. Some immigrants are more than qualified to fill the void. If they speak multiple languages and have international experience, so much the better.

Individuals and societies too often still play what has been termed a "zero-sum game." That attitude assumes there are limited resources in the world and we're all in competition for them. What you get, I don't get, and vice versa. But innovation and adaptation are our greatest human strengths. If we learn to use these qualities to increase resources, we all win. Immigrants can be a big part of that way forward.

REFERENCES

1. Segal, R, Raglan, L, Rank, O. Introduction: In Quest of the Hero. *Quest of the Hero.* 1990; Princeton, N.J.: Princeton University Press

2. Sullivan P, Young Adult Literature: Everyone a Hero: Teaching and Taking the Mythic Journey, *The English Journal.* 1983; 72(7):88–90.

3. United Nations Department of Economic and Social Affairs, *news release.* 09/17/2019. https://news.un.org/en/story/2019/09/1046562

4. United Nations High Commissioner for Refugees (UNHR). Global Trends: Forced Displacement 2019; UNHCR 2020. http://www.unhcr.org/refugee-statistics

5. ESPMI Network. Reconceptualizing refugees and force migration in the 21st century. May 26, 2015. https://refugeereview2.wordpress.com/

6. International Organization for Migration. *Irregular Migrant, Refugee Arrivals in Europe Top One Million in 2015.* https://www.iom.int/news/irregular-migrant-refugee-arrivals-europe-top-one-million-2015-iom

7. Eurostat News Release 48/2020. *612,700 first-time asylum seekers registered in 2019, up by 12% compared to 2018.* March 20, 2020.

8. International Organization for Migration. *Venezuela Refugee and Migrant Crisis.* 2020. https://www.iom.int/venezuela-refugee-and-migrant-crisis

9. US Census Bureau. *Net Migration between the U.S. and Abroad Added 595,000 to National Population Between 2018 and 2019.* December 30, 2019. https://www.census.gov/library/stories/2019/12/net-international-migration-projected-to-fall-lowest-levels-this-decade.html

10. Carrasco, F dJ V. El vía crucis del migrante: demandas y membresía (The migrant via crucis: demands and membership). *Trace* 2018; 73:117–133.

11. International Committee of the Red Cross, *Central American Annual Report, 2019.* https://www.icrc.org/en/document/central-america-annual-report-2019

12. Eurostat. *Migration and migrant population statistics: statistics explained.* May 2020. https://ec.europa.eu/eurostat/statistics-explained/index. php?title=Migration_and_migrant_population_statistics

13. US Department of State – Bureau of Consumer Affairs. *Visas.* https:// travel.state.gov/content/travel/en/us-visas/immigrate/employment-based-immigrant-visas.html

14. United Nations High Commissioner for Refugees (UNHR). Refugees. https://www.un.org/en/global-issues/refugees

15. Noe-Bustamante L, Mora L, Lopez M H. *About One-in-Four U.S. Hispanics Have Heard of Latinx, but Just 3% Use It.* 2020; Pew Research Center.

16. Barnhouse AH, Brugler CJ, Harkulich JT. Relocation stress syndrome. *Nurse Diagnosis.* 1992; 3(4):166–168.

17. Berry, J. W., & Kim, U. Acculturation and mental health. In P. R. Dasen, J. W. Berry, & N. Sartorius (Eds.), *Cross-cultural research and methodology series, 1988; Vol. 10. Health and cross-cultural psychology: Toward applications* (p. 207–236). Sage Publications, Inc.

18. American Psychiatric Association. *Diagnostic and statistical manual of mental disorders: DSM-IV-TR.* 2000; Washington, DC: Author.

19. American Psychiatric Association. *Diagnostic and statistical manual of mental disorders (5th ed.).* 2013; Arlington, VA: Author.

20. World Health Organization. *The ICD-10 classification of mental and behavioural disorders: Clinical descriptions and diagnostic guidelines.* 1992; Geneva: World Health Organization.

21. Ghanem-Ybarra, G.J. *The acculturation process and ethnic self-identification of second generation Christian Palestinian American women.* (Unpublished doctoral dissertation), 2003; California Professional School of Psychology at Alliant International University, San Diego.

22. Cervantes RC, Padilla AM, Napper LE, Goldbach JT. Acculturation-Related Stress and Mental Health Outcomes Among Three Generations of Hispanic Adolescents. *Hispanic Journal of Behavioral Sciences,* 2013; 35(4):451–468.

23. Reimann JOF, Ghulam M, Rodríguez-Reimann DI, Beylouni MF. Project Salaam: Assessing mental health needs among San Diego's greater Middle Eastern and East African communities. *Ethnicity & Disease. 2007 Summer; 17(2 Suppl 3):S3-39-S3-41.*

24. Montgomery, J. (1996). Components of Refugee Adaptation. *The International Migration Review. 1996; 30(3):679–702.*

25. Ye, HD, Muhamad, HJ. Acculturative Stress Level Among International Postgraduate Students of a Public University in Malaysia. *International Journal of Public Health and Clinical Sciences.* 2017; 4(4):2289–7577.

26. Berry JW. Acculturation. In the *Encyclopedia of Applied Psychology*, 2004; 27–34. Academic Press, Elsevier: Amsterdam.

27. Berry, JW. Theories and models of acculturation. In S. J. Schwartz & J. B. Unger (Eds.), *Oxford library of psychology. The Oxford handbook of acculturation and health, 2017;* (p. 15–28). Oxford University Press.

28. Berry, J. W., Kim, U., Minde, T., & Mok, D. Comparative studies of acculturative stress. *International Migration Review. 1987;* 21:491–511.

29. Perez, RM Linguistic Acculturation and Context on Self-Esteem: Hispanic Youth Between Cultures, *Child and Adolescent Social Work Journal.* 2011; 28(3):203–228.

30. Smokowski, PR, Roderick R, Martica LB. "Acculturation and Latino Family Processes: How Cultural Involvement, Biculturalism, and Acculturation Gaps Influence Family Dynamics." *Family Relations. 2008;* 57(3):295–308.

31. Phinney, J., & Haas, K. The process of coping among ethnic minority first-generation college freshman: a narrative approach. *The Journal of Social Psychology.* 2003; 143:707–726.

32. Tajfel, H., & Turner, J. C. (1986). The social identity theory of intergroup behavior. In S. Worchel & W. G. Austin *Psychology of Intergroup Relations.* 1986; 7–24. Nelson-Hall: Chicago, IL.

33. American Psychological Association. *Discrimination: What it is, and how to cope.* October 31, 2019. https://www.apa.org/topics/racism-bias-discrimination/types-stress

34. American Psychological Association, *Stress in America 2020.* https://www.apa.org/news/press/releases/stress/2020/report-october

35. European Agency for Fundamental Rights. *Second European Union Minorities and Discrimination Survey: Main Results; 2017* https://fra.europa.eu/sites/default/files/fra_uploads/fra-2017-eu-midis-ii-main-results_en.pdf

36. Gonzalez-Barrera A & Lopez, MH. Before COVID-19, many Latinos worried about their place in America and had experienced discrimination. Pew Research Center. *FACTANK*, July 22, 2020. https://www.pewresearch.org/fact-tank/2020/07/22/

before-covid-19-many-latinos-worried-about-their-place-in-america-and-had-experienced-discrimination/

37. United States Department of Housing and Urban Development, *Fair Housing Act.* https://www.hud.gov/program_offices/ fair_housing_equal_opp/fair_housing_act_overview

38. US Civil Rights Act of 1964. https://www.dol.gov/agencies/oasam/ civil-rights-center/statutes/civil-rights-act-of-1964

39. US Equal Employment Opportunity Commission. The Age Discrimination in Employment Act. https://www.eeoc.gov/statutes/ age-discrimination-employment-act-1967

40. US Americans with Disability Act. https://www.ada.gov/cguide. htm#anchor62335

41. Lui PP, Quezada L. Associations between microaggression and adjustment outcomes: A meta-analytic and narrative review. *Psychological Bulletin.* 2019; 145(1):45–78.

42. *Washington Examiner.* https://www.washingtonexaminer.com/ washington-secrets/report-illegal-immigration-leads-to-2-200-deaths-118-000-rapes-138-000-assaults

43. Child soldiers. United Nations International Children's Emergency Fund. https://www.unicefusa.org/stories/ unicef-working-free-child-soldiers-around-world/35474

44. Perreira KM, Ornelas I. Painful Passages: Traumatic Experiences and Post-Traumatic Stress among Immigrant Latino Adolescents and their Primary Caregivers. *International Migration Review.* 2013; 47(4):976–1005.

45. Nesterko Y, Friedrich M, Brähler E, Hinz A, Glaesmer H. Mental health among immigrants in Germany - the impact of self-attribution and attribution by others as an immigrant. *BMC Public Health.* 2019; 19(1):1697.

46. Bas-Sarmiento P, Saucedo-Moreno MJ, Fernández-Gutiérrez M, Poza-Méndez M. Mental Health in Immigrants Versus Native Population: A Systematic Review of the Literature. *Archives of Psychiatric Nursing.* 2017; 31(1):111–121.

47. The Soufan Center. *Syria: The Humanitarian-Security Nexus,* 2017, Author.

48. Friedman, AR. Rape and domestic violence: the experience of refugee women. In Cole, E., Espin, OM, & Rothblum, ED. *Refugee Women and their Mental Health.* 1992; Harington Park Press: Binghamton: NY

49. Reimann JOF, Christopher R. *The Traumatic Event Sequelae Inventory (TESI): Administration, Scoring, and Procedures Manual (Second Edition).* Sparks, NV. 2016; Professional, Clinical and Forensic Assessments, LLC.

50. Schnyder U, Bryant RA, Ehlers A, Foa EB, Hasan A, Gladys G, Kristensen CH, Neuner F, Oe M, Yule W. Culture-sensitive psychotraumatology. *European Journal of Psychotraumatology.* 2016; 7:31179.

51. Hinton DE, Lewis-Fernández R. The cross-cultural validity of posttraumatic stress disorder: implications for DSM-5. *Depression and Anxiety.* 2011; 28(9):783–801.

52. Hinton DE, Pich V, Marques L, Nickerson A, Pollack MH. Khyâl attacks: a key idiom of distress among traumatized Cambodia refugees. *Culture, Medicine and Psychiatry.* 2010; 34(2):244–78.

53. Anxiety. American Psychological Association. https://www.apa.org/topics/anxiety

54. Lewis-Fernández R , Gorritz M , Raggio GA , et al: Association of trauma-related disorders and dissociation with four idioms of distress among Latino psychiatric outpatients. *Culture, Medicine and Psychiatry. 2010*; 34(2):219–243.

55. Forte A, Trobia F, Gualtieri F, Lamis DA, Cardamone G, Giallonardo V, Fiorillo A, Girardi P, Pompili M. Suicide Risk among Immigrants and Ethnic Minorities: A Literature Overview. *International Journal of Environmental Research and Public Health.* 2018; 15(7):1438.

56. United Nations Office of Drugs and Crime. *Statistics: Drug use.* https://www.unodc.org/unodc/en/data-and-analysis/statistics/drug-use.html

57. Dydyk AM, Jain NK, Gupta M. *Opioid Use Disorder.* 2020 Nov 20. In: StatPearls [Internet]. 2021; Treasure Island (FL): StatPearls Publishing.

58. Centers for Disease Control and Prevention. *Overdose Deaths Accelerating During COVID-19.* Press Release. December 17, 2020. https://www.cdc.gov/media/releases/2020/p1218-overdose-deaths-covid-19.html

59. Murray, K & Parisi, T. *Addiction and Refugees and Immigrants.* Addiction Center. March 2, 2020. https://www.addictioncenter.com/addiction/refugees-immigrants/

60. Manghi, R, Broers, B. Khan, R. Benguettat, D. Khazaal, Y. Zullino, DF. Khat use: lifestyle or addiction. *Journal of Psychoactive Drugs.* 2009; 41(1):1–10.

61. Salas-Wright CP, Vaughn MG, Clark TT, Terzis LD, Córdova D. Substance use disorders among first-and second-generation immigrant adults in the United States: evidence of an immigrant paradox? *Journal of Studies on Alcohol and Drugs.* 2014; 75(6):958–967.

62. National Institute on Alcohol Abuse and Alcoholism. *Module 10F: Immigrants, refugees, and alcohol.* In Social work education for the prevention and treatment of alcohol use disorders. Washington, D.C. https://slideplayer.com/slide/3841167/

63. Woodward AM, Dwinell AD, Arons BS. Barriers to mental health care for Hispanic Americans: a literature review and discussion. *Journal of Mental Health Administration.* 1992; 19(3):224–36.

64. American Psychiatric Association Fact Sheet: Mental Health Disparities: Hispanics and Latinos. https://www.psychiatry.org/psychiatrists/cultural-competency/education/hispanic-patients

65. Reimann JOF, Ghulam M, Rodríguez-Reimann DI, Beylouni MF. *Bringing communities together for wellness: An assessment of emotional health needs among San Diego's Middle Eastern, North African, and East African groups.* 2005; San Diego: ICSD.

66. Tahirbegolli B, Çavdar S, Çetinkaya Sümer E, Akdeniz SI, Vehid S. Outpatient admissions and hospital costs of Syrian refugees in a Turkish university hospital. *Saudi Medical Journal.* 2016; 37(7):809–12.

67. Physicians for Human Rights. 2000. https://secure.phr.org/

68. Centers for Disease Control and Prevention. *BCG-Vaccine Fact Sheet.* https://www.cdc.gov/tb/publications/factsheets/prevention/bcg.htm

69. United States Drug Enforcement Agency. *Fact Sheets. Rohypnol.* https://www.dea.gov/factsheets/rohypnol

70. Lara M, Gamboa C, Kahramanian MI, Morales LS, Bautista DE. Acculturation and Latino health in the United States: a review of the literature and its sociopolitical context. *Annual Review of Public Health.* 2005; 26:367–397.

71. Rodríguez-Reimann DI, Nicassio P, Reimann JOF, Gallegos PI, Olmedo EL. Acculturation and health beliefs of Mexican Americans regarding tuberculosis prevention. *Journal of Immigrant Health,* 2004; 6:51–62.

72. Shapiro K, Gong WC. Natural products used for diabetes. *Journal of the American Pharmacists Association.* 2002; 42(2):217–226.

73. Liu J, Shi JZ, Yu LM, Goyer RA, Waalkes MP. Mercury in traditional medicines: is cinnabar toxicologically similar to common mercurials? *Experimental Biology & Medicine (Maywood)*. 2008; 233(7):810–817.

74. Vickers AJ, Vertosick EA, Lewith G, MacPherson H, Foster NE, Sherman KJ, Irnich D, Witt CM, Linde K; Acupuncture Trialists' Collaboration. Acupuncture for Chronic Pain: Update of an Individual Patient Data Meta-Analysis. *The Journal of Pain*. 2018; 19(5):455–474.

75. Gutiérrez Á, Young MT, Dueñas M, García A, Márquez G, Chávez ME, Ramírez S, Rico S, Bravo RL. Laboring With the Heart: Promotoras' Transformations, Professional Challenges, and Relationships With Communities. *Family & Community Health*. 2020; Dec 4.

76. Barlow, S. Understanding the Healer Archetype https://susannabarlow.com/on-archetypes/understanding-the-healer-archetype/

77. d'Artis Kancs, Patrizio Lecca Long-term Social, Economic and Fiscal Effects of Immigration into the EU: The Role of the Integration Policy 2017 European Commission, JRC Technical Reports

78. Kosten D. Immigrants as Economic Contributors: Immigrant Tax Contributions and Spending Power. *National Immigration Forum*. https://immigrationforum.org/article/immigrants-as-economic-contributors-immigrant-tax-contributions-and-spending-power/

79. Courthouse News Services. New Americans in San Diego: A Snapshot of the Demographic and Economic Contributions of Immigrants in the County https://www.courthousenews.com/wp-content/uploads/2018/02/immigrant-contributions.pdf

80. Welcoming San Diego. https://www.sandiego.gov/welcomingsd

81. National Academies of Sciences, Engineering, and Medicine. The Economic and Fiscal Consequences of Immigration. Washington, DC: The National Academies Press. 2017. https://doi.org/10.17226/23550.

82. US Bureau of Labor Statistics. TED: The Economics Daily, May 24, 2017 https://www.bls.gov/opub/ted/2017/foreign-born-workers-made-83-point-1-percent-of-the-earnings-of-their-native-born-counterparts-in-2016.htm

83. Reimann, JOF. *Factors of culture, socioeconomic status, minority group membership, and gender in the career choice flexibility of Mexican Americans on the U.S.-Mexico Border: A structural model*. Dissertation Abstracts International: Section B: the Sciences & Engineering. Vol. 57(9-B), March 1997. Available through WorldCat. https://www.worldcat.org/

84. Krumboltz, JD. The wisdom of indecision. *Journal of Vocational Behavior.* 1992; 41:239–244.
85. Etzel JM, Nagy G, Terence JG, Tracey TJG. The Spherical Model of Vocational Interests in Germany. *Journal of Career Assessment.* 2015; 24 (4):701–717.
86. Alegría M, Mulvaney-Day N, Torres M, Polo A, Cao Z, Canino G. Prevalence of psychiatric disorders across Latino subgroups in the United States. *American Journal of Public Health.* 2007; 97(1):68–75.
87. Arnetz J, Rofa Y, Arnetz B, Ventimiglia M, Jamil H. Resilience as a protective factor against the development of psychopathology among refugees. *Journal of Nervous and Mental Disease.* 2013; 201(3):167–72.
88. American Psychological Association. *Crossroads the psychology of immigration in the new century.* Report of the APA presidential task force on immigration. 2012.
89. Chiswick, BR, Miller W. The "Negative" Assimilation of Immigrants: A Special Case. *Industrial and Labor Relations Review.* 2011; (64)3:502–525.
90. Hayes-Bautista, DE, Hsu P, Hayes-Bautista M, Iñiguez D, Chamberlin, CL, Rico C, Solorio R. An Anomaly Within the Latino Epidemiological Paradox. The Latino Adolescent Male Mortality Peak. *Archives of Pediatrics & Adolescent Medicine.* 2002; 156:480–484.
91. Smith DP, Bradshaw BS. Rethinking the Hispanic paradox: death rates and life expectancy for US non-Hispanic White and Hispanic populations. *American Journal of Public Health.* 2006; 96(9):1686–92.
92. Goleman D. *Emotional Intelligence: Why It Can Matter More Than IQ.* 1995 Bantam Books: New York New York
93. US Health & Human Services, Office of Minority Health. *Cultural competence described.* https://minorityhealth.hhs.gov/omh/browse. aspx?lvl=1&lvlid=6
94. Freimuth, VS, Quinn, SC, Thomas, SB, Cole G., Zook E., Duncan, T. African Americans' views on research and the Tuskegee Syphilis Study. *Social Science & Medicine.* 2001; 52:797–808.
95. Lackland DT, Sims-Robinson C, Jones Buie JN, Voeks JH. Impact of COVID-19 on Clinical Research and Inclusion of Diverse Populations. *Ethnicity & Disease.* 2020; 30(3):429–432.
96. Reimann JOF, Talavera GA, Salmon M, Nuñez J, Velasquez RJ. Cultural competence among physicians treating Mexican Americans

who have diabetes: A structural model. *Social Science & Medicine.* 2004; 59:2195–2205.

97. Reimann, JOF, Rodríguez-Reimann, DI. (2010) Community based health needs assessments with culturally distinct populations. In A. Pelham & E. Sills (Eds.) *Promoting Health & Wellness in Underserved Communities: Multidisciplinary Perspectives through Service Learning Series* (pp.82–100), Sterling, VA: Stylus Publishing.

98. US Health & Human Services, Office of Minority Health. The National CLAS Standards. https://minorityhealth.hhs.gov/omh/browse.aspx?lvl=2&lvlid=53

99. Mews C, Schuster S, Vajda C, et al. Cultural Competence and Global Health: Perspectives for Medical Education - Position paper of the GMA Committee on Cultural Competence and Global Health. *GMS Journal for Medical Education.* 2018; 35(3):1–17

100. US Department of Health & Human Services, Office of Disease Prevention & Health Promotion. *Healthy People 2020.* Disparities Section https://www.healthypeople.gov/2020/about/foundation-health-measures/Disparities

101. Reimann JOF, Ghulam M, Rodríguez-Reimann DI, Beylouni MF. *Bringing communities together for wellness: An assessment of emotional health needs among San Diego's Middle Eastern, North African, and East African groups.* 2005, San Diego: ICSD.

102. Reimann JOF, Rodríguez-Reimann DI, Medina M. *Proyecto Salud Libre: An assessment of the mental health needs in Imperial County's communities.* 2006; Brawley, CA: Clinicas de Salud del Pueblo.

103. Reimann JOF, Rodríguez-Reimann DI, Talavera GA. *Cultural competence in the licensure of health care professionals. Final Report to the US Department of Health & Human Services*, Office of Minority Health 2003

104. Cooper-Patrick, L, Gallo, JJ, Gonzales, JJ, Vu, HT, Powe, NR, Nelson, C, & Ford, DE (1999). Race, gender, and partnership in the patient-physician relationship. *Journal of the American Medical Association*, 1999; 282:583–589.

105. Komaromy, M, Grumbach, K, Drake, M, Vranizan K, Lurie N, Keane D, Bindman AB. (1996) The role of black and Hispanic physicians in providing health care for underserved populations. *New England Journal of Medicine*, 1996, 334:1305–1310.

106. Hayes-Bautista, DE (1997). Workforce issues and options in the border states. *Journal of Border Health.* 1997; 4:12–20.

107. Dawson-Saunders B, Iwamoto CK, Ross L, Volle RL, Nungester, RJ Performance on the National Board of Medical Examiners. Part I Examination by men and women of different race and ethnicity. *The Journal of the American Medical Association.* 1994; 272(9):674–9

108. Swanson DB, Bowles LT. Letter to the editor. *Evaluation & the Health Professions.* 1996; 19(2):412–419.

109. Werner, E. A review of the Examination for Professional Practice in Psychology. 1991; Sacramento: California Department of Consumer Affairs.

110. Kelsey, SL & Werner E. An analysis of factors associated with adverse impact in the July 1985 registered nurses licensing examination. 1986 Sacramento CA: California Department of Consumer Affairs.

111. Nowrasteh, A. Illegal Immigrants and Crime – Assessing the Evidence. Cato Institute. March 4, 2019. https://www.cato.org/blog/illegal-immigrants-crime-assessing-evidence

112. Ousey, GC, Kubrin, CE. (2018). "Immigration and Crime: Assessing a Contentious Issue". *Annual Review of Criminology.* 2018; (1):63–84.

113. Sampson RJ. Rethinking crime and immigration. *Contexts. 2008;* 7(1):28–33.

114. Sydes, M. Immigration, Ethnicity, and Neighborhood Violence: Considering Both Concentration and Diversity Effects. *Race and Justice.* 2019 09-18.

115. Bianchi, M. Buonanno, P. Pinotti, P. "Do Immigrants Cause Crime?" *Journal of the European Economic Association.* 2012; 10(6):1318–1347.

116. Donato Di Carlo, D, Schulte-Cloos, J, Saudelli G. Has immigration really led to an increase in crime in Italy? *European Politics and Policy or the London School of Economics.* March 3, 2018.

117. Banks, James (2011-05-01). "Foreign National Prisoners in the UK: Explanations and Implications." *The Howard Journal of Criminal Justice.* 2011; 50(2):184–198.

118. Alonso, C., Garoupa, Nuno; Perera, Marcelo; Vazquez, Pablo. Immigration and Crime in Spain, 1999–2006. FEDEA. 01/01/2008.

119. Mohdin, Aamna. "What effect did the record influx of refugees have on jobs and crime in Germany? Not much". *Quartz.* Retrieved 2017-02-03.

120. Skarðhamar, Torbjørn; Thorsen, Lotte R.; Henriksen, Kristin (12 September 2011). Kriminalitet og straff blant innvandrere og øvrig befolkning [Crime and punishment among immigrants and non-immigrants] (PDF) (in Norwegian). 2019; Oslo: Statistics Norway. pp. 9–28.

121. Mastrobuoni, Giovanni; Pinotti, Paolo (2015). Legal Status and the Criminal Activity of Immigrants. *American Economic Journal: Applied Economics.* 2015; 7(2):175–206.

122. United Nations Office of the Special Representative of the Secretary-General on Sexual Violence in Conflict. *Report – Somalia.* June 3, 2020. https://www.un.org/sexualviolenceinconflict/countries/somalia/

123. American Civil Liberties Union. *Human Trafficking: Modern Enslavement of Immigrant Women in the United States.* 2020. https://www.aclu.org/other/human-trafficking-modern-enslavement-immigrant-women-united-states

124. Samuel Fikiri Cinini. A Victimological exploration of the victimisation vulnerability of a group of foreign nationals in the city of Durban, 2015, Masters of Social Sciences Thesis, School of Applied Human Sciences, Department of Criminology and Forensic Studies, University of KwaZulu-Natal

125. Bove, V; Böhmelt, T. Does Immigration Induce Terrorism? *The Journal of Politics.* 2016; 78(2):572–588.

126. US Department of Homeland Security, National Terrorism Advisory System. *Bulletin.* January 27, 2021 https://www.dhs.gov/sites/default/files/ntas/alerts/21_0127_ntas-bulletin.pdf

127. Horgan, J.G. (2017). Psychology of terrorism: introduction to a special issue. *American Psychologist,* 2017; 72:199–204.

128. Merari, A. Driven to death: Psychological and social aspects of suicide terrorism. 2010; Oxford, UK: Oxford University Press.

129. Victoroff, J. The mind of a terrorist: A review and critique of psychological approaches. *The Journal of Conflict Resolution.* 2005; 49:2–42.

130. Gupta, D.K. The leadership puzzle in terrorism study. In U. Kummar & M.K. Manddal (Eds.). *Countering terrorism: psychosocial strategies.* 2012; (pp. 143–160) New Delhi, India: Sage Publications.

131. Ellis, H.B. & Abdi, S.M. Building community resilience to violent extremism through genuine partnership. *American Psychologist,* 2017; 72:289–300.

132. Twenge JM, Joiner TE. US Census Bureau-assessed prevalence of anxiety and depressive symptoms in 2019 and during the 2020 COVID-19 pandemic. *Depression and Anxiety*. 2020; (37)10:947–1059.

133. Pollard MS, Tucker JS, Green HD Jr. Changes in Adult Alcohol Use and Consequences During the COVID-19 Pandemic in the U.S. *JAMA Network Open*. 2020; Sep 1;3(9).

134. Torales J, O'Higgins M, Castaldelli-Maia JM, Ventriglio A. The outbreak of COVID-19 coronavirus and its impact on global mental health. *International Journal of Social Psychiatry*. 2020; Jun;66(4):317–320.

135. Gelatt J. Migration Policy Institute. *Fact Sheet. Immigrant Workers: Vital to the U.S. COVID-19 Response, Disproportionately Vulnerable.* March 2020. https://www.migrationpolicy.org/research/ immigrant-workers-us-covid-19-response

136. Migration Policy Institute. *The central role of immigrants in the US food supply chain.* April 2020. https://www.migrationpolicy.org/content/ essential-role-immigrants-us-food-supply-chain

137. Panjwani, A. UK has one of the highest levels of foreign-born doctors and nurses in the EU. *Full Fact*, December 2, 2019. https://fullfact.org/ health/foreign-born-nhs-eu/

138. Dempster H & Smith R. *Immigrant health workers are on the Covid 19 frontline. We need more of them.* Center for Global Development. https://www.cgdev.org/blog/ migrant-health-workers-are-covid-19-frontline-we-need-more-them

139. Amnesty International, Global: *Amnesty analysis reveals over 7,000 health workers have died from COVID-19*, 3 September 2020, https://www.amnesty.org/en/latest/news/2020/09/ amnesty-analysis-7000-health-workers-have-died-from-covid19/

140. Ewing W. Immigrant healthcare workers play a vital role in the United States COVID–19 response. *Immigration Impact*. March 24, 2020 https://immigrationimpact.com/2020/03/24/health-care-workers-covid19-immigrants/#.YRG09ohKiHt

141. Smith, Y. *Physician Shortage* https://www.news-medical.net/health/ Physician-Shortage.aspx

142. Global Skills Partnership. Center for Global Development. https://www.cgdev.org/page/global-skill-partnerships

GLOSSARY

Acculturation is generally defined as cultural modification and adaptation of an individual, group, or people by learning and integrating traits and norms from another culture. Acculturation is not a one size fits all concept in that it can take many forms.

Acculturation Stress refers to the psychological challenges involved in adapting to a new culture. This stress can be significant especially when acculturation involves major life changes like learning a new language, reduced socioeconomic status, facing discrimination in a new country, etc. Acculturation stress has been acknowledged as an area of clinical concern in the International Classification of Diseases, Tenth Revision, (ICD-10) and the Diagnostic and Statistical Manual of Mental Disorders, Fifth Edition (DSM–5).

Anglo generally refers to people who are native English-speaking inhabitants of the Americas. It is a term often used by Latinos to described white people native to the US, though that is not the exclusive application of the expression.

Anxiety is an emotional condition often marked by fear, nervousness, agitation, worry, and restlessness. If not extreme and/or persistent, anxiety can be a normal part of life. But more severe anxiety that interferes with activities of daily living can warrant a clinical diagnosis and require treatment. More substantial anxiety can result in panic attacks that include such physical symptoms as shortness of breath, increased heartbeat, sweating, tingling sensations, nausea, and digestive distress.

Assimilation (Cultural) is the process by which an immigrant and/or minority group takes on the values, behaviors, and beliefs of the dominant culture within a country or region. Unlike some other forms of acculturation, assimilation generally presumes that the process also involves the loss of cultural norms, beliefs, habits, and values people had previously espoused.

Asylum is a term used in the context of refugees who have been granted a specific legal immigration status in a country they have entered. To be granted asylum people have to show that they were persecuted in the past, or that they have a well-founded fear of being persecuted in the future should they return to the country of origin. People fleeing their homes, often in a hurry, do not tend to have much formal documentation about the threats they were under.

Cultural Competence: The US Office of Minority Health defines this as "having the capacity to function effectively as an individual and an organization within the context of cultural beliefs, behaviors, and needs presented by consumers and their communities." Internationally, cultural competence research and advocacy also emphasizes global health. As such it seeks to understand the interconnections between regions, cultural groups, climate change, ecosystems, and political realities as they impact health and wellness.

Deferred Action for Childhood Arrivals (DACA) is (as of this writing) a US immigration policy that allows some immigrants who have not committed crimes and were brought to the US as children to be given a deferment that keeps them from being deported and allows them to work in the US To be eligible for the program, recipients cannot have felonies or serious misdemeanors on their records. It does not provide a path to citizenship. The policy was implemented by then-President Barack Obama on June 15, 2012. DACA has been a point of contention in US politics, and the future of immigrants falling into DACA's criteria remains uncertain.

Depression is a mental disorder often characterized by sadness, social isolation, problems sleeping, crying spells, loss of interest in various activities that were pleasurable in the past, decreased physical energy, reduced self-confidence, difficulties focusing and concentrating, as well as a host of other symptoms. In more severe circumstances it can lead to suicidal ideas and even completed suicide. Depression can be caused by environmental stress/personal problems, biological/genetic factors, serious physical illness, medication side effects, and the aftermath of the pregnancy. Some episodes can be short and transient while others occur over and over again.

Discrimination is a basic behavior that arises from biases and prejudices. It is the unjust treatment of groups of people. Discrimination can target a variety of such groups based on their race, skin color, gender, national origins, sexual orientation, disability, religion, and many other factors.

Ethnic Identity is the degree to which a person identifies with a particular ethnic group or groups. This has been postulated as including the way we understand, label, and feel about the group we identify with as well as other groups. It tends to be reflected in the actions we take around these issues. In short, it is how we see ourselves and our place in society. It is not static but can change as you mature and gain new experiences. The concept can be broadened to "cultural identity" which includes sexual orientation, religion or spirituality, socioeconomic status, and many other groupings.

Emotional Intelligence is the capacity to be aware of, control, and express one's emotions effectively. Strong emotional intelligence increases the chance that a person will be able to handle interpersonal relationships thoughtfully and with empathy. Emotional intelligence is often thought to have five basic components: self-awareness, self-regulation, internal motivation, empathy, and social skills.

Foreign National is a person who has citizenship in a foreign country.

Foreign students are those who come to study in a foreign country under a particular educational visa. In the US, this can be an F-1 or M-1 visa. Students who study in a country other than their own often do so with the premise that they will return home when the studies are done.

Generational Status refers to how long an individual or family unit has been in a country. If you are foreign-born you are considered "the first generation." If your parents were born in a foreign country but you were not, you are "the second generation."

The Health Belief Model (HBM) is a social/psychological construct that seeks to explain and predict health-related actions. The HBM suggests that people's beliefs around health problems, perceived benefits of action, barriers to such action, and self-efficacy explain why they will or will not engage in healthy behaviors. Our research has found that the various parts of the HBM are all important. But how they connect and interact with each other can vary from culture to culture.

Highly Integrated Bicultural is a type of acculturation in which persons keep relevant practices from their country of origin but also adopt practices from their new country. In other words, people maintain some degree of home-culture integrity. At the same time, they learn how to participate as a vital part of their new country's larger social network. This has the potential to be a "best of both worlds" approach.

Home Country is the country that people originated from (e.g., by birth, Citizenship, etc.)

Host Country is the new country immigrants have entered.

An immigrant is a person who has come to live permanently in a country that is not his place of birth and/or citizenship. The key here is the word "permanently." As such, it does not apply to people who are tourists or who visit a foreign county for work temporarily.

Immigrant Paradox (aka "Latino paradox" or "Hispanic paradox") refers to research showing that first-generation immigrants tend to have health outcomes that are roughly equivalent to (or sometimes better than) their native-born counterparts. This is considered a paradox because first-generation immigrants often have lower average income and education, factors that are generally connected with worse health and higher mortality rates across the world.

A Migrant is a person who is moving from one place country to another. This is sometimes applied to people who come to a foreign county to work (e.g., migrant farmworkers) with the possible intent to periodically return home.

Nopales is the Spanish word for *Opuntia cacti* (prickly pear cactus). Nopales are frequently part of a Mexican diet and are reputed to be good for people who have diabetes. Several peer-reviewed research studies have found that *nopales* can help with glycemic control. As such, it is an example of effective traditional practice.

Perceived Discrimination is not meant to imply that people's experiences of discrimination and racism are untrue. The term "perceived" is sometimes used in research because it is perceptions (awareness) that tend to drive attitudes and behavioral strategies.

Personality Disorders are mental illnesses that involve long-term patterns of inflexible and dysfunctional thoughts and behaviors. They can cause serious and repeated problems in all aspects of a person's life including

GLOSSARY

relationships and work. People with personality disorders are often flighty and volatile and have trouble maintaining any long-term relationships.

Posttraumatic Stress Disorder (PTSD) is a mental condition that is triggered in some people because they have experienced or witnessed a terrifying event (e.g. war experiences, sexual assault, a major car accident, an industrial accident with significant injuries). Common symptoms can include intrusive thoughts about the event, severe anxiety, flashbacks to the event, avoiding anything that reminds people of the event, nightmares, depression, difficulties thinking and concentrating, and withdrawal from others. PTSD can be quite common in refugees or soldiers who have had bad experiences in war.

Promotora (aka Community Health Worker) is an often-self-taught Latino community member and leader who provides health advice in the neighborhood. This has been a common tradition for some time. Professional researchers and providers now tend to seek out promotoras because they have the ear of their community. They often train these individuals in public health and employ them as liaisons to get needed information about prevention, treatment, and related services out. The basic concept of a Community Health Worker is not limited to Latinos. We have used a similar approach with Middle Eastern and East African populations.

A Refugee is someone who has been forced to migrate out of her country of origin because of threats to him or herself. This term is a bit tricky because it is sometimes broadly applied to any immigrant who was forced to migrate. But on a more formal basis, it tends to refer to a specific legal status. For example, according to title VIII of the United States Code Section 1100 and 1A 42, a refugee is an alien who is unable or unwilling to return to his or her country because of persecution, or a well-founded fear of persecution, on account of race, religion, nationality, membership in a particular social group, or political opinion. An alien cannot qualify for this status if he or she has persecuted others, has been firmly resettled in a third country, or has been convicted of a certain serious crime. The specific legal parameters around refugee status tend to vary from country to country.

Traditional in the context of this book refers to the cultural and national norms an immigrant experienced in his or her country of origin. In the acculturation context, some people choose to maintain such norms and traditions and remain relatively separate from the broader society of their adopted country.

Trauma can include physical injuries, psychological distress, or some combination of both. Physical trauma refers to a clinically serious injury to the body. Most often this is divided into "blunt force trauma" when something strikes but does not necessarily penetrate the body. This can cause concussions, broken bones, and similar injuries. "Penetrating trauma" refers to circumstances in which some object has pierced the body's skin, usually resulting in an open would. Psychological trauma refers to cognitive and emotional disturbances that can arise from one or more distressing events (e.g., war, domestic violence, auto, and industrial accidents, sexual abuse, and exploitation). Directly experiencing or even witnessing such events often causes overwhelming stress that a person cannot cope with. In many incidents, physical and psychological trauma happens together. Also, some people experience "cumulative trauma" which involves not one but a protracted set of harmful events. An example on the physical side is carpal tunnel syndrome. In the psychological realm, an unrelenting series of negative experiences can increase distress. This can be the case even if the individual events are, in and of themselves relatively minor (as in microaggression).

INDEX

ACKNOWLEDGEMENTS

Many people have directly or indirectly shaped the content of this book. Mr. William Romo and Ms. Dolores J. Rodríguez provided essential feedback on our initial drafts. Ms. Leticia Gloria did much of the research on the family history of Mr. Felipe Romo. Our editor Ms. Leslie Schwartz, helped us find the right style for you, the reader. She also asked important questions about our topics that we had not thought of otherwise. In addition, we are grateful to Mr. David Wogahn who guided us through the many complex pieces involved in publishing a book.

We also wish to acknowledge the friends and colleagues who worked with us on projects cited in this book. Most centrally, these include our friend and partner, Dr. Harve S. Meskin, Co-Founder of the Group for Immigrant Resettlement and Assessment (GIRA) as well as Dr. Mehboob Ghulam, Dr. Fouad Beylouni, Ms. Maria Elena Patiño, Ms. Aida Amar and Dr. Gregory Talavera. We have also appreciated our work with leaders in the local East African communities, particularly Mr. Ahmed Sahid, President and CEO of Somali Family Service of San Diego and Mr. Abdi Mohamoud, President and CEO of the Horn of Africa organization.

Most importantly, we wish to thank our many patients and clients who shared their life stories with us over the years. They cannot be named here due to confidentiality regulations. But their experiences are at the heart of both this book's content and our motivation to write it.

ABOUT THE AUTHORS

Joachim "Joe" Reimann, Ph.D. was born in Berlin, Germany. His family immigrated to the US when he was 10 years old. At present Joachim is a clinical psychologist and President of the Group for Immigrant Resettlement and Assessment. He has a long history of working with immigrant communities and is a former Board Chair for Somali Family Services of San Diego. While previously on the adjunct faculty at San Diego State University's Graduate School of Public Health, Joachim received grant support from the US Office of Minority Health, the National Center for Minority Health Disparities, and the Hispanic Centers of Excellence. His research has been published in *Social Science & Medicine*, *The American Journal of Preventive Medicine*, *Ethnicity & Health*, the *Journal of Clinical Psychology* and other outlets. Joachim's doctorate also has an emphasis area in Organizational Psychology. Consequently he has been part of various workforce development projects and held management positions in local government and the private sector over his career. This allows him to better understand immigrant issues around career and employment.

Dolores I. Rodríguez-Reimann, Ph.D. was born in Piedras Negras, Mexico. Her family immigrated to the US when she was 15 years old. A bilingual & bi-cultural (English/Spanish) psychologist, Dolores has worked with immigrant and refugee populations for many years. Specific venues include private clinical practice, contracted services through Survivor of Torture International, and funded research. At present, Dolores is an executive with the Group for Immigrant Resettlement and Assessment. While an adjunct faculty member at San Diego State University's Graduate School of Public Health, she received grant and contract support through the National Heart, Lung & Blood Institute (NHLBI), the National Cancer Institute (NCI), and the US Office of Minority Health. Her research on acculturation and related issues has been published in *Ethnicity & Disease* and the *Journal of Immigrant Health*. Dolores has also served in multiple organizational leadership positions over her career.